What others *bigger than you.*

"*bigger than you.* is a must read for any entrepreneur serious about leading a scalable and sustainable business that provides freedom and financial security for years to come. Kelly provides the blueprint to bypass the start-and-stop trap that challenges many entrepreneurs on the way to the top."
~ Ashley Crouch
Founder Appleseed Communications

"*bigger than you.* shows you exactly what to do as a business owner to instantly increase your profits, sanity and freedom."
~ Dustin Mathews
Wealth Evangelist & Entrepreneur VIP Contributor

"*bigger than you.* lays out the exact blueprint to step into the CEO role of your business and get it running like a well-oiled machine."
~ Mariana Ruiz
Founder, Impact Driven Entrepreneur

"In her new book, *bigger than you.*, Kelly Roach unlocks the secret of long-term, sustainable success for entrepreneurs who have become the roadblock to their own company's growth. Chock full of real-life stories and Kelly's valuable personal experience, this is one investment that will pay you back many times over in the coming years."
~ Peter Economy
The Leadership Guy, INC.COM

bigger than you.

The Entrepreneur's Guide to Building an Unstoppable Team

By Kelly Roach

Business Growth Strategist | Speaker | Peak Performance Coach

bigger than you.
The Entrepreneur's Guide to Building an Unstoppable Team

Published by Primedia E-launch LLC

Copyright © 2018
All rights reserved. No part of this book may be reproduced, stored in a retrieval system, or transmitted in any form or by any means without the written permission of the publisher. Printed in the United States of America.

ISBN-13: 978-1727587265

Cover design by Cathy Peluso

DISCLAIMER AND/OR LEGAL NOTICES
While the publisher and authors have used their best efforts in preparing this book, they make no representations or warranties with respect to the accuracy or completeness of the contents of this book. The advice and strategies contained herein may not be suitable for your situation. You should consult a professional where appropriate. Neither the publisher nor the authors shall be liable for any loss of profit or any other commercial damages, including but not limited to special, incidental, consequential, or other damages. The purchaser or reader of this publication assumes responsibility for the use of these materials and information. Adherence to all applicable laws and regulations, both advertising and all other aspects of doing business in the United States or any other jurisdiction, is the sole responsibility of the purchaser or reader.

This book is intended to provide accurate information with regards to the subject matter covered. However, the Author and the Publisher accept no responsibility for inaccuracies or omissions, and the Author and Publisher specifically disclaim any liability, loss, or risk, whether personal, financial, or otherwise, that is incurred as a consequence, directly or indirectly, from the use and/or application of any of the contents of this book.

*To my team: You are the ones behind this dream —
thank you!*

About Kelly Roach

Kelly Roach is known internationally as an "Authority for entrepreneurs and business leaders who want more success, freedom, and fulfillment in their lives." Her work has been featured in *INC*, *Entrepreneur*, on ABC, NBC and countless other media outlets and publications around the world.

She has already directly helped thousands of individuals master sales, marketing, and business growth strategies to increase their incomes and achieve their goals.

Kelly started her career with a Fortune 500 firm where she was promoted seven times in eight years, becoming the youngest Senior Vice President in the firm. Kelly's experience hiring, training, coaching, and managing individuals across 17 locations and managing a team of over 100 individuals up and down the East Coast prepared her for her entrepreneurial journey.

After breaking every record in the company's history for profit, growth, sales, and expansion, coupled with millions in profit added to the bottom line, Kelly knew it was time to focus on helping others do the same.

Kelly's number one passion in life is helping others succeed with the right strategies, action plan, and mindset for success. Kelly's company, **Kelly Roach Coaching** helps entrepreneurs, business owners and executive leaders achieve rapid, sustainable business growth in record time (without compromising their quality of life or sanity along the way).

Kelly does private consulting with corporations and small business owners, runs online training and coaching programs for entrepreneurs, and hosts her own Elite Mastermind for individuals who are seriously committed to transformative results in their business and life.

About Kelly Roach

To learn how you can work with Kelly and her team, email coaching@kellyroachcoaching.com or visit www.kellyroachcoaching.com to connect with us today.

Table of Contents

Introduction 3

What Freedom? 7

The Quicksand Hell of a Duct-Taped Team 23

You Can't Fire Everyone 37

Reverse the Cycle 47

Still Broke? 67

Remove the #1 Bottleneck to Growth 77

Step Up and Lead… or Die 95

Six Pillars of Effective Leadership 103

The Only Path to True Wealth and Entrepreneurial Freedom .. 129

Transform and Launch! 135

Resources 141

About the Author 143

Acknowledgements 147

Introduction

First of all, I know that deep down, if you are reading this book, you have a big vision for yourself, your business, and your life. You started your business because you have a dream of creating financial abundance for yourself and your family, living your highest purpose and bringing immense value to the world doing it. You have a dream of creating ultimate freedom and the flexibility to put your family first, just like I did when I started.

What I am about to reveal to you in this book includes how I enabled my husband to retire when our daughter was born, paid off our dream house in three years, and became millionaires living debt free at a very young age… all while working fewer than 40 hours a week in my business. And what I will tell you is that **none** of it could have been accomplished without a dream team.

The first thing you probably learned as you launched your business and became an entrepreneur is that none of the rules you may have learned up until this point in your life apply. Suddenly, you find yourself in a wild jungle, and everything you thought you knew, you have to re-learn… sometimes the hard way!

No doubt the first lesson you learned was that "that thing" – the core of your business, that you are so good at – becomes much less important, overshadowed by the need to market yourself and your business to generate leads and close sales.

However, the second big lesson of entrepreneurship, and exactly why I'm writing this book, is that even if you master lesson one (sales and marketing) you still have a very high likelihood of failure, burnout, and never achieving your dreams of financial independence unless you master lesson number two.

Lesson number two is: Your business's ongoing success depends on your ability to surround yourself with a winning team. If you want to experience true and lasting freedom, you must be able to both grow your business and still maintain your quality of life.

Let's face it. There are only so many hours in any given day or week that you can realistically dedicate to your business. Even if you were to forego having a personal life, dedicating 14 or more hours to your business every day, your mental capacity would wane (regardless of your caffeine intake!), resulting in less than a stellar performance in your business. Your customers or clients would certainly notice, and you would most likely be giving up on most of the reasons why you started your business in the first place.

There is no way to sustainably grow a business year after year, and do so profitably, without taking on greater and greater working hours unless you have a winning team.

You need a group of people as dedicated to the dream as you are, both willing and able to go all in on helping you make it happen!

The key to attracting and retaining the right people is, in a nutshell, leadership. When it comes to leadership, as my friend, Gerard Adams always says, "The hard work comes before the dream."

A fair word of warning as we get started: Leadership and developing a winning team around you is not a "quick and easy" process… there are no shortcuts. In fact, it is a process with which most entrepreneurs get frustrated and give up on, throwing in the towel long before they get anywhere near the success they initially envisioned.

I want you to be excited and committed to the process you are about to embark on because when you master the lessons, strategies, and mindset I am about to share, you will unlock your unlimited potential and be shocked at what you can accomplish.

Having a winning team is literally the act of multiplying yourself in your business with only one difference: You are surrounding yourself with people who can do things better, faster, and smarter than you can, creating breakthroughs you never believed possible.

As you start reading this book, the biggest thing to understand and realize is that the only thing that stands between where you are right now and making all of your dreams come true is having the patience to persevere through this process.

It's not "out there," so to speak. It is inside of you… in your head and your heart. I encourage you, as you read through this book, to keep a strong focus on the person in the mirror. By doing so, you will get the most out of this book, and it is how you are going to change your business and, indeed, your life as a result of the lessons I'm about to share.

So let's begin, shall we?

Introduction

Chapter One:
What Freedom?

To all the business owners and entrepreneurs out there, looking at the business they've created – pouring into it their blood, sweat, and tears – perhaps investing thousands or tens of thousands of dollars along with countless hours away from family and any semblance of a personal life who may now be thinking that they've been sold the proverbial bill of goods… this book is for you. There is light at the end of the tunnel; you just have to make sure you are building the right kind of tunnel….

When it comes to entrepreneurship, unless you approach it with an engineer-like precision in the way you construct the foundation of your business, you are going to struggle… immensely. (Why doesn't anyone tell us this before we start our companies, right?)

Without implementing very specific systems for

- sales
- marketing
- people
- operations
- and even managing your money…

… it is a very quick and easy threshold to cross from your business being a catalyst for achieving your dreams to being a lead weight around your ankles.

By the time many of my coaching clients come to me for help, their business is in the chaos and pandemonium stage rather than providing them the platform they need to achieve their goals and live life on their terms.

It is important to know that no matter where you are starting today, you can turn it around, tighten it up, and make changes to take your business from struggling to skyrocketing quickly with the strategies you will learn throughout this book.

I am about to share powerful stories of entrepreneurs who I've helped transform so that you can learn from them and hopefully avoid similar mistakes and instead expedite and streamline your own transformations and awakenings.

(The "names have been changed to protect their privacy" since the stories may be sensitive.)

Let's start with Charlie. Charlie came to me, having started his business three years earlier. He had a big dream and a goal to launch a juice company to be a champion of health bringing clean, innovative products to the market.

He'd already invested over $100,000 in resources, assets, programs, coaching, and online tools for his business. However, he had never aligned himself with a coach who helped him understand that infrastructure is everything. Charlie's business lacked a solid sales and marketing system, staff, or infrastructure to facilitate growth.

He launched his business with the idea that his dedication to creating quality juice would be enough. The heart of his business would lie in the best fruits and vegetables and his recipes.

Charlie figured his incredible passion about espousing good health would be enough of a foundation. He never envisioned that becoming a master of generating leads and closing sales would be necessary. Nor did he figure on having to build a team that could ultimately mirror his passion and handle this part of the business for him. He didn't realize that without these things, his big vision would never become reality.

By the time Charlie called me, he was close to $100,000 in debt, didn't have a single paying client, and had no idea what to do or where to turn… other than to give up on his dream or start over completely.

With the stress and anxiety of not knowing where to turn or what to do, Charlie's personal life was in shambles. Plus, this champion of good health was losing sleep and gaining weight. His stress level was through the roof, and it seemed a panic attack loomed around every corner. As for the credit card bills that rolled in every month, he struggled just to pay the minimum, and of course with that, the compounding interest also compounded his stress level and worry. Charlie had also returned to working full time for someone else, just to try to keep his head above water and make the monthly minimum payments.

> *If you fail to focus on what moves the needle in your business, you'll always be asking, "What freedom?" when it comes to being your own boss.*

This entrepreneur had big passions and big dreams. He was not afraid of working hard; however, his focus was misplaced. Charlie was spending all of his time and money on things that would never enable him to achieve what he wanted no matter how hard or how long he worked… and no matter how good his juices were.

On our very first call, he shared that he was considering yet another $30,000 investment in a new piece of equipment. I see this so often. As new entrepreneurs, we think if we just have the right office, equipment, technology and website, we just have to be set up for success... right?!

Unfortunately, none of these things that seem like necessities is going to put money in the bank and keep a roof over your head.

In the beginning, every ounce of energy and focus needs to be spent on building an engaged audience, an email list that converts (sales and marketing), and systems to support the business in running like a well-oiled machine, but many times, we focus on everything but....

Building a team to help him generate leads and close wholesale clients to get his product in the hands of millions of consumers was not even a thought, although he had already spent more than it would cost to do so on things that didn't move the needle.

Reading this you may say, "WOW, that is so obvious. I would never make a stupid mistake like that." But slow down there ranger... we all do.

It's true. If you do not have ongoing outside counsel in your business, it's guaranteed that you are regularly making decisions that if you were looking at someone else's business, you would immediately yell, "STOP!"

This is another reason why I am so thankful for the opportunity to coach, mentor, and train entrepreneurs around the world to leverage, scale, and grow.

Like them, I'm certain you already have the power and energy invested to do it; you just need to do the right things in the right order and in the right way to get the desired result.

I'm happy to share that, working together with Charlie, we simplified everything he was doing and focused on the infrastructure of his business.

By leveraging social media and the online strategies I teach in the Unstoppable Entrepreneur program, he began generating sales and revenue almost immediately with zero overhead other than his time – which, guess what, he was already spending anyway, but on all the wrong things.

Slowly Charlie worked his way out of debt and into profitability. No matter where you are versus where you want to be, you can too! Just remember you need to spend your time and money on the things that make a real difference in your bottom line, and if you don't know how or what or where, then get started by finding someone to teach you.

Like Charlie, if all of your money is invested in things other than building a team that can sell, market and serve your clients and customers for you, it's time to take a hard look at that.

One Thing Changes Everything

In so many aspects of building our businesses and getting to our goals, we try to work harder and harder and longer and longer, making things more complex than they need to be. So often, we resort to relying on blunt force to get to where we want to be. We fall victim to doing the same things repeatedly and expecting a different result.

Instead of taking time at the outset to build a business from the inside out, we end up rushing ahead only to find ourselves building it from the outside in.

Once this is the case, no matter how hard and long you work, you'll tend to invest in things that are not essential to your operation and profitability... and you're never going to get the results you want until you take the time to fix it.

We all can have a tendency to avoid addressing the really hard part of running our business. We end up focusing on everything else but that! It's easier to wrap ourselves up in what comes naturally, is habit, or within our comfort zones. What is that one thing that can change everything? Leadership.

Leadership is never convenient. It is never the thing that any entrepreneur wants to slow down and spend time on. It's a skill that many ignore rather than hone.

> *Leadership changes everything. It is the key to ultimate and lasting freedom.*

Leadership will never feel like it is the most urgent thing on which you should be spending your time and effort. You may have a hard time convincing yourself that this is a skill set that you need to develop. However, leadership – or lack thereof – is one of the hidden things that will grind your business to a halt and prevent you from ever moving forward.

You can address leadership proactively, as a part of your growth process (both your business and personal growth) starting right now, or you can wait until you're backed into a corner with everything around you either stuck or falling apart.

Sadly, there are many entrepreneurs who shut down or lose their businesses altogether before they ever focus on developing a leadership skill set or even realize that such a skill set is necessary for success.

bigger than you.

Effective leadership is a key ingredient; however, it's often overlooked because it feels so intangible. As such, it doesn't appear to be the "needle mover" when, in fact, it is the very thing that can swing a business from wild success to ultimate failure or vice versa. This "intangible" is what can and will change everything for ***you!***

Freedom? Really?

Remember all the great things you envisioned when you decided to take a chance on ***you*** by starting your own business?

- Working from anywhere
- Setting your own hours
- Traveling the world
- Getting paid what you're worth
- Making a real and lasting difference in the world

Chances are, before you got started you did your research and knew – and had hard data that proved – the world needed what you were about to offer.

You probably spent hours doing market research and still have your written SWOT analysis in which you figured out all of your strengths, weaknesses, opportunities, and threats. You learned everything there was to know about your competitors. You knew everything there was to know about your target audience and really drilled down to their specific demographics and psychographics.

Then you launched, knowing that you would now be your own boss. You could and would set your own hours, working anytime and anywhere. No longer would you be chained to a cubicle, answering to someone else and keeping someone else's schedule. Nope. You were now going to call the shots. Right?

Perhaps you've heard the phrase, "Then life got in the way." Well, I'm betting that once you launched your company, you quickly learned that "business got in the way." Suddenly there were all of these other tasks that, while necessary to run a successful business, have nothing to do with your core competency whether you're running a physician's office, weight loss firm, wealth management company, or any number of service- or product-based businesses – the list could go on forever.

You quickly realize that you have **no freedom**. Instead of working anywhere or anytime, you find yourself working everywhere and all the time. Yeah, but you're working for yourself, so that's okay, right? You may convince yourself of that; however, you're chained to your business in the same way you may have been chained to your 9-to-5 job. In all likelihood, your hours aren't even 9-to-5 any longer. They're probably more like 6:00 to 8:00… and that's 6:00 a.m. to 8:00 p.m. – not cool.

Working those hours may work in the beginning, but I assure you, it is unsustainable; it's only a matter of time before the burnout and breakdown happen.

Suddenly you're backed into a corner, frozen by a combination of indecision and exhaustion. You're too tired to think straight and your indecision or the poor decisions you make as a result simply complicate and exacerbate the problem. It's a really nasty Catch-22. You have nowhere to turn and no resources left because you've already invested everything you have.

bigger than you.

Simplification

Here is the really good news: Everything can be simplified. Every successful business has streamlined processes, systems, and the right people that allow the business to be profitable. This does not mean things always flow perfectly and that problems don't arise, but it means there are reinforcements in place to prevent them from spiraling.

Take a look at the processes you have in place now, and think about how you got to where you are now and how those processes came to be. Consider this scenario and see if it might ring true for you.

You want to go from point A to point C. When you hit point B, the bridge is out, so you have to take a detour that leads you to point D. At point D, there's roadwork and the construction crew redirects you to point E. Once there, you're out of gas, so you have to push the car to the gas station at point F. There is actually no road between F and your original destination at point C, so you have to proceed to point G to pick up a road that leads to point H, that may finally, finally get you back to point C.

It's a harrowing trip and it's become very, very complicated. In looking back, if perhaps you'd taken time to build that bridge at point B, it would have been far simpler… and probably faster. Enter building a winning team and the importance of leadership.

This is a great example of how "business gets in the way" and how your processes and infrastructure can follow a similar convoluted path to achieve the outcome you want. Your business has become an unbelievably complicated beast. You look around and think, "Holy sh*t. I'm in this alone. I have no help or support. I'm backed into this corner. I can't grow because I can't work any more hours."

Here's the real rub: You cannot even begin to delegate some of the tasks if you want to because your business is so disorganized and disjointed that it barely makes sense to **you** anymore, let alone someone new. If you do hire someone, the complexity of the infrastructure you've created precludes them from achieving success.

> *Unless you delegate, you can never grow your business. Unless you simplify your processes, you can never delegate.*

Until you simplify your business, you will not have employees who can effectively contribute to getting the job done, let alone to do so profitably.

Consider John. He launched his graphic design business. He's really creative and flat out brilliant at what he does. He's built up his client base successfully; however, clients all seem to have last minute changes and rush jobs, so he's always bouncing from one project to another and struggling to get anything finished **and** invoiced.

He tends to be very haphazard about tracking his hours on any given project and he loathes paperwork. John tries to keep a rough tally in his head about how much time he spends on any project, or if he's quoted a total at the start, he figures he doesn't have to keep track of his time.

The problem is that clients keep asking for additional work or making changes that are outside the scope of his original estimate. He's failing to capture that, effectively leaving money on the table and driving his effective hourly rate to minimum wage or lower. John's always procrastinating on invoicing, which leads to a very serious, business-threatening cash flow problem. He knows he should hire someone to do the invoicing, but his lack of any sort of timekeeping infrastructure makes that impossible. It's all in his head, and what's in his brain is an inaccurate mishmash anyway. It's out of control. John's in real trouble.

John was a client of mine who was on the brink of being out of business when we got started because things had gotten so out of control, it seemed more manageable to quit than it was to unravel the mess.

Here is what we did:

1. We got a proper legal contract in place for each job he took with specific clauses and pricing to handle scope creep and additional revisions beyond the original agreement... and reinforced it.
2. We got his billing process systematized and, although he could not automate due to the nature of the work, he got as close to this as possible with certain checkpoints each week, and he hired someone to help with invoicing.
3. We raised his rates and redesigned his packages so that he was focusing clients on specific recurring packages for ongoing needs versus one-off, a la carte items that created a roller coaster effect in his income.
4. We hired a part-time designer to support him on the more basic design elements that could easily be transferred, which he could easily pay for now that he was billing clients timely, charging more, and had ongoing agreements versus hourly jobs with no ongoing income attached.

The result?

Within 90 days, John was able to eliminate 20+ hours from his workweek... and get on a regular sleep schedule and close to double his actual net take-home income.

We focused on three things: systems, team, and the way he was positioning his packages and pricing, and this literally transformed his income and quality of life in a matter of days.

It can happen for you, too.

So many times I see entrepreneurs resisting hiring because it's "too expensive" when in reality, when managed properly, it will make you money not cost you money to have help. You are already spending the money in other ways... you just don't realize it.

It's All in Your Head

If you've created one work-around solution to a problem and then created a work-around to the work-around... and around and around and around... you probably realize that you're in a very tough position for someone to come in and help you.

Entrepreneurs who reach this point finally understand that they can't do it alone, and you will need to SLOW DOWN and step back so that you can get things set up the right way.

When it's all in your head, you might quickly come to that age-old conclusion: "It's easier to do it myself than explain it to someone else." Well, of course it is!

bigger than you.

But with that attitude and mindset, you'll never grow, will never really be profitable, and will continue to be chained to your business 24/7/365.

The first step, before you can move forward and implement anything that I am going to share with you to scale your business with ease is to get it out of your head and into documented systems and processes.

You have to take the time to define your vision and the processes and plan to attain that vision. Determine what people and resources will be needed along with defining and organizing the systems that will support your endeavor. Then document it! Only with documentation can you bring someone in and have them work in your business efficiently and effectively. Give them a set structure and a step-by-step process for them to follow for everything you need them to do. Your goal must be to create a precise, predictable, and **repeatable** result.

This must be your goal in order to get out of the problem of the business stopping every time you stop. Slowly pull it out of your head and into a tangible form. Create a system and a structure for everything that you do… A to Z! With systems and structure, work is transferrable, and other people can be quickly and easily onboarded. The onboarding process – how easy or difficult it is – is the true barometer of how well a company is run. If it's easy and efficient, chances are excellent that you're looking at a highly profitable company and lucrative business model that can be sustained and that can scale.

If onboarding is difficult, it makes it harder to hire, far more expensive and much more challenging to make employees successful. You want a documented process for why you do what you do that's set up in such a way that

19

anyone can come in, learn the process, and get repeatable results.

You must have this in place before you can even think about building engagement and inspiring your team. You have to get really clear about the pillars of profitability in your business and the levers that are going to drive sustainable growth. Organize. Systematize. Document.

There are two primary scenarios that I see most often in "small businesses" that keep people stuck. Either they're so disorganized that they can't even consider hiring someone, or they have a staff but the lack of organization is leading to the turn-and-burn cycle in which there's a revolving door of turnover that spins pretty fast. Everyone they hire is a disappointment and no one can meet their expectations. Whether they're quick to get rid of the employee or the employee is quick to head for the exit doesn't matter. The cause and the end result are the same.

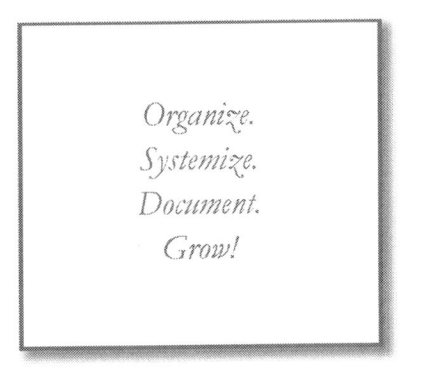

Organize.
Systemize.
Document.
Grow!

There Is Hope!

If you're reading this thinking "How did things get so out of control," I want to know there is hope! I want you to know that freedom is completely attainable for you. Your business can be what you dreamed it would be, being both financially abundant and allowing you to have the personal life you want, putting your family first, with time freedom. However, this doesn't happen by chance. It will only happen by design… and it starts today with being intentional about the way you are going to structure and run your company going forward.

If you find yourself in John's shoes, with a company that has evolved into a complex beast, there is hope. If you are willing to read this book and employ the lessons I share and take the appropriate and necessary action, you can create a business that you control rather than one that controls you. If you're willing to try something new, I assure you that everything is still possible, and it will not take you years and years to achieve what you want. <u>Simplify first, then organize, then document your systems, and you will begin to grow.</u>

If you feel like you can barely breathe reading this first chapter and you are saying to yourself, "Holy hell, that sounds just like me! I need an intervention," that's a good thing. It means you are now ready to begin your total business transformation and finally create true and lasting entrepreneurial freedom, just like my Legacy Leaders are doing each day. (My Legacy Leaders program is a CEO development program that helps entrepreneurs become stellar impactful leaders so that they can transition from "being the business" to "running the business")

> *"If your actions inspire others to dream more, learn more, do more and become more, you are a leader."*
> *~ John Quincy Adams*

Action Items:

1. Take time to reflect on the vision you first had for your business when you launched it. Jot down everything you thought you would achieve both in your business and also how that would then affect your personal life and family.

2. Rank where you are in terms of your vision on a scale of 1 - 10 (1 = I should close shop and go back to work for someone else; 10 = I'm killing it, so I should stop reading this book right now.)

3. Next, write down some of the things that fall into the category "business got in the way" (the tasks you handle every day or week that are taking too much of your time without contributing to growth). Get a plan to offload them right away.

4. Designate a few hours each week to begin documenting your processes and actually put it on your calendar. What are the top five areas of the business that take the most time, that if systematized and delegated would be life changing for you? Start there. Pay attention to what you can simplify and just get started!

To learn how to put everything we discuss in this book into *action* right away, go to www.kellyroachcoaching.com/influence and watch the free, life-changing training now!

Chapter Two:

The Quicksand Hell of a Duct-Taped Team

Perhaps you remember (or have seen) those 60s-era B-movies that always featured some hapless character being sucked to their death in quicksand. The more they struggled, the worse it got for them. While the catastrophic effects of quicksand might be hyped up for dramatic tension in movies, the negative effects are quite real if you duct tape a team together.

Ask any successful leader, CEO, or entrepreneur about how they managed to rise to the top and maintain their success, and you will invariably hear the same answer. The number one reason they cite is their team – the winning team they built. When most entrepreneurs launch their businesses, leadership and team building are often the furthest things from their mind. These don't seem sexy and exciting, worthy of attention, and they're not the topics of conversation that entrepreneurs want to have. In fact, team building doesn't hit the radar for most entrepreneurs until they're suffering extreme burnout by trying to do it all themselves… until they are backed into a corner and faced with a crisis, requiring them to take a step to get help.

Unfortunately, I see this occur in countless entrepreneurs with whom I've worked around the world and across the dozens and dozens of industries and vertical markets that they represent. If you find yourself in this situation, you have a lot of company. Consider this analogy: You have a great car that you want to drive from Philadelphia

The Quicksand Hell of a Duct-Taped Team

to San Francisco, but you're only planning to add fuel when you reach your destination. Obviously, the car needs gas in order to move at all. Fuel cannot be an afterthought. That may seem overly simplistic, but I've often seen a parallel entrepreneurial mindset: "I will invest in a team when I get six figures in revenue... or when I'm hitting my take-home income goals... or when I achieve XYZ milestone." There is no shortage of checkpoint expectations that I've heard. It's akin to planning to gas up after you've arrived. It's always, "I'll hire a team when...."

However, when "when" occurs is almost always at a critical juncture; things are moving fast and you cannot afford to make mistakes yet this is exactly what happens. Panic and pressure lead to bad hiring decisions mixed with a lack of preparedness to onboard with no one to train properly as the cherry on top... and we all know how this story ends.

Let's be clear: <u>its team that drives growth</u>. Growth does not drive your need for a team. My goal in writing this book is to help change the entrepreneurial mindset around how teams can drive growth in your organization if you're willing to invest and grow and do it the right way. And how to use team building as the catalyst that makes your business truly a freedom-based business that provides you with the income and time freedom you desire rather than a trap that keeps you stuck in the rat race forever.

> *Team drives growth... not the other way around!*

There are many, many entrepreneurs who have a team around them, yet they still feel overworked and underpaid because they have a team that's been duct taped together rather than one that's been built intentionally and by design. Whether you find yourself in that situation or are just starting on the path of building your team, I want to guide you through the process, so you avoid the dreaded quicksand.

The one thing that all of my most successful clients whom I have helped to make six- and even seven-figure leaps in their businesses have in common is that they understand that it's the team that allows them to live the dream. They understand that hiring the right people, investing in them, and elevating them is the number one most important role of the CEO in any organization, and anyone, if committed, can learn this process.

(If this is totally new to you and you want to learn the A-Z system I teach for attracting, building, and leveraging a dream team for massive success, quickly go to
www.kellyroachcoaching.com/mastermind
to learn about my Legacy Leaders program.)

What Color Is Your Duct Tape?

These days, duct tape comes in assorted colors and patterns, and people make all sorts of creations with it. Yes, duct tape can be useful, but not when it comes to building a coherent team that will enable to you drive your business and grow your enterprise. So take the following quiz and see which one applies to your situation:

> A. You haven't hired a soul yet and are doing it all yourself. You're burned out and your dream of running your own business is turning nightmare-ish.

B. You use a series of 1099-contracted vendors who come and go as they please, do what they want when they want, and may or may not be reliable to complete the task that you hired them for... when you need them the most. Yeah, not being responsible for payroll taxes seemed like a good idea to go this route, but when you're left trying to piece it all together, well....

C. You're a client of a done-for-you service, but they are not your team and may not align with your mission. They probably don't even know what your mission is. They simply send you the canned information... and an invoice. They're not a team member; you're a client.

D. You've hired outside the country and are paying pennies on the dollar for a VA on an hourly basis. Although $300/month sounded like a deal, you spend five times that amount wasting time trying to get through the communication barrier and time zone differential.

E. You've hired friends or family. If you've been down this road, you know it can quickly backfire on multiple fronts, and the result is bad for your business and can make holiday meals rather strained.

F. You've attempted an internal employee or two... or maybe even five, but it's been a constant cycle of hire/fire/burnout/slide back. (More on this in Chapter 3.)

G. You have long-term employees, but they've never really bought into your vision, don't follow procedures, aren't willing to invest in the company, and are stuck in the way they've always done things and have no interest in change. These folks merely clock in and clock out.

H. You have an unstoppable dream team with internal talent that owns their area of responsibility, drives superior results, and you can count on them to further your mission!

> *"No man will make a great leader who wants to do it all himself, or to get all the credit for doing it."*
> *~ Andrew Carnegie*

Unless you found yourself answering "yes" to the last one, keep reading.

The vast majority of entrepreneurs aren't completely alone in running their businesses; however, they feel completely isolated and alone. It's the old, "It's lonely at the top" sort of thinking. This stems from the fact that most don't have relationships with others who are invested in their mission, committed to growth, and willing to do whatever it takes to push the organization's goals and aspirations forward. If you find yourself feeling a sense of isolation – and even loneliness – in your business, I assure you, the reason is because you have a duct-taped team. There can be plenty of people around you, along with the associated payroll expenses, but because of the nature of the foundation you created (or failed to create), you don't have anyone who is truly *on your team*.

So What Is an Unstoppable Dream Team?

I want to clearly define this for you so that you better understand why what you've been doing so far hasn't worked or isn't working to:

A) Help you achieve your income and family goals, or

B) Experience the entrepreneurial freedom you want and deserve.

Both of these *are* completely attainable. In fact, they are inevitable when you build an unstoppable dream team. However, you must also be willing to look in the mirror to determine the changes you will have to make as the business owner and leader in order to cross that bridge to freedom.

An unstoppable dream team can begin with one or more individuals who are profit focused, completely and totally invested, flexible, adaptable, and engaged in working as hard at your mission for profitability, growth, and success as you are.

If you just read that definition and thought, "That's never going to happen. It's butterfly and fairy dust thinking," that's exactly what I am going to unpack and demonstrate for you throughout the rest of this book, so keep reading.

Let me take a moment to share with you my own dream team who fill this bill and enable me to be unstoppable. I have three long-term team members who are truly a dream team and many others "in the making."

Stephanie, Nicole, and Lindsay are full-time, internal employees.

They continually go above and beyond, are always thinking outside the box – and looking for ways we can grow faster, serve more deeply, and make a bigger difference.

They show up to online company events even when they're off the clock and on personal time because they simply want to be a part of it and to bolster their own education to improve client interface, put in extra hours without being asked, and… they simply care.

> *"Leadership is the ability to get extraordinary achievement from ordinary people." ~ Brian Tracy*

The number one bit of feedback I receive from my clients is that they're blown away by the integrity, care, and kindness they receive from my team. Even in the sales process, when my team is closing a client, that client typically reports that it was the best sales experience they've ever had – they don't feel that they've been "sold to," even though they may have landed in one of our multi-thousand-dollar, high-ticket programs.

These three dream team members each have other team members on their "team within the team" that they are responsible for cultivating, onboarding, and helping to grow into the next generation of dream team members.

The characteristics they all have in common include:

- Flexibility
- Adaptability
- Profit focused/results driven
- Contribute daily to the bottom line
- Go above and beyond daily without being asked
- Treat their role in the company as their own "small business" in which they own their career
- Proactive problem solvers
- High integrity

Hire the Right DNA

Before we go any further, I want to caution you: A lot of entrepreneurs think that to create a dream team, they have to go out and hire super high level, industry experts that they could never afford or who would otherwise be unwilling to work for them because their level of expertise far exceeds the salary opportunity presented. This is a broken mindset! It is completely incorrect to think that to build an unstoppable team you have to break the bank or go deep into debt.

Of course, with any hire, it is going to take time for you to get that person up to speed, productive, and profitable, but you don't have to look for an industry expert, thinking that you can shorten the learning curve. In fact, as I hope you noticed as I described my own team, I mentioned nothing about skill set... because it's not about skill set. Skills can be learned. Character, integrity, and work ethic are the things that make up the DNA of an unstoppable dream team.

bigger than you.

It's all about the intangibles an employee brings to the table – their level of caring and dedication – more so than their skills. Dream team employees want to be part of something extraordinary.

> *"Ability is what you're capable of doing. Motivation determines what you do. Attitude determines how well you do it."* ~ Lou Holtz

When it comes to hiring, keep this in mind: M&A trumps S&K every single time. Look at someone's motivation and attitude and determine how that may or may not fit into your organization rather than assessing what their skill and knowledge may be. You can always teach skill and knowledge to a willing student; however, motivation and attitude come from within. Your employees have to bring that to the table. If they don't have it, you're better off moving on to the next candidate, no matter how much of an industry expert someone might be.

Are You Carrying Everyone?

Having read this far, it should be becoming abundantly clear that a part-time employee or an outside contractor can never and will never become the catalyst for growth in your organization.

Most entrepreneurs are type-A personalities with a high level of work ethic, which accounts for a lot of their success; however, this can hurt more than it helps when it comes to team building. Too often, I see business owners working diligently to make an unworkable situation work! They're "head down" focused on getting results rather than "head up" analyzing how they're trying to go about it and realizing that their approach might not be the smartest, most efficient and effective one to get the results they really want.

I had a client who had a team of staff members, but she was still working 80 hours a week, was burned out, and definitely at her breaking point. The business was bringing in almost $1 million in revenue but her expenses were in the very high $900,000s, leaving very little profit left over. She had six team members, but couldn't truly say that she was getting results from any of them, so she turned to me to help her determine what would be the logical next step. Close the business? Sell the business? Improve the business… but how? With a quick review of her P&L (profit and loss statement), I could see that money was incorrectly allocated, and not only was there overspending on the wrong types of positions, she was also using outside contractors that she couldn't really manage… legally or otherwise. It was actually killing her business because she was not able to drive profitable results and growth although she was spending almost a million dollars to run the business!

Failure resulted from mismanagement of people, and the team members weren't right for her type of business; they were also too heavily weighted on services and client care without enough allocated toward positions that would generate revenue and profit. In going through a process of re-focusing who and how she managed, including onboarding new internal staff rather than external contractors, we alleviated some of the pressure that fell entirely on her shoulders to be the salesperson and sole revenue generator.

Her personal sales were supporting the incomes of seven different people. It was definitely out of balance!

This situation, unfortunately, is pretty typical. "Business owner as the only sales person" is a syndrome I see a lot. Business owners keep adding additional staff, but that exacerbates the pressure on them personally to generate more sales to cover the additional head count. Every time they hire, that expense comes out of the company's profitability and ultimately out of the business owner's pocket. It is another vicious Catch-22 in which the entrepreneur thinks that the only way to grow is to hire more, but they're hiring the wrong people or people in the wrong positions, and the more that happens, the harder and harder the business owner has to work to generate revenue. Whew. No wonder they're burned out!

Back to Simplification

As with processes and procedures, the solution is often found in simplification – less is more. If you find that your attention is scattered all over the place with contractors, part-time employees, and outsourced services, you are actually spending far more than you need to without getting the best results. Instead, you'll be better served and more profitable if you would have that one "right-hand person" who can actually be you initial core team member and who can begin to allow you to reverse the cycle of burnout and stop the Catch-22 of you working solely to cover the paychecks of other people. When you find and hire this person, you can also avoid the need to work additional hours (if you even have hours to spare!) every time you take on a new client.

Many times, what you think is saving you money or you believe is the work-around solution to avoid hiring a full-time staff person (or a contractor fully dedicated to you) is actually allowing money to pour out of your business. Again, simplification and really committing to one person is very, very likely the right solution. Commit to one person, so they will commit to you. I find some entrepreneurs have this idea that their employees should be more committed to them than they are to their employees. Honestly, you can only and should only expect the level of commitment from an employee that you are willing to make to that person. If your commitment falls in the realm of spending a few hundred bucks a month for them to work a few hours for you, why would you expect them to invest their heart, soul, and mind into your business?

This problem – inequity of commitment – is really at the root and heartbeat of the quicksand hell of a duct-taped team. You simply cannot fail to invest and then rely on a hope and a prayer that you'll have an unstoppable team. We are each responsible for the success or failure of our businesses, and we must be willing to invest first!

Recap:

- ➢ If you wait until you experience growth to hire a team, you've waited too long. Team drives growth; growth does not drive the need for team.
- ➢ If you're feeling like "it's lonely at the top," take another look at who is on your team. Does this need to change?
- ➢ An unstoppable dream team can begin with one or more individuals who are profit focused, completely and totally invested, flexible, adaptable,

and engaged in working as hard at your mission for profitability, growth, and success as you are. They don't need to come into the business with a high level of expertise, but you do need the work ethic, integrity, and values that you want representing your firm.
- Hire for motivation and attitude rather than skill and knowledge.
- "Business owner as the only salesperson" is an unsustainable model and will quickly burn you out.
- There must be equitable commitment: You must be as committed to your employees as you expect them to be to you.

Action Items:

1. List your "I will hire when" excuses, and it's time to let them go!

2. Determine where you are in terms of building a team:
   - ❏ Hired no one
   - ❏ Use 1099-contractors
   - ❏ Client of a done-for-you service
   - ❏ Hired off-shore
   - ❏ Using friends and family as employees
   - ❏ Hired and fired repeatedly
   - ❏ Have long-term employees, but they do not constitute an unstoppable dream team

   What does your next step need to be to get growing right away?

3. Consider what DNA you want and need in your company. List the characteristics that are most important to you.

4. If you have employees, how do you rank their motivation and attitude? List their names and rank them 1-10 (1 = They're taking up space and oxygen; 10 = They are true impact players who are generating growth and profitability).

To learn how to put everything we discuss in this book into *action* right away, go to
www.kellyroachcoaching.com/influence
and watch the free, life-changing training now!

Chapter Three:

You Can't Fire Everyone

If I had a dollar for every entrepreneur who comes to me and says, "I need help with my team. I always want to fire everyone…," I'd be retired already.

There's a phenomenon in the small business and entrepreneurial communities that is driven by how and why we go into business in the first place. Most people launch their business because they uncovered their passion and something that they love doing and want to focus on that full time, or they couldn't bear the thought of working for someone else for one more day, or they were the best at their craft and didn't believe they were being justly compensated for their expertise.

Ninety-nine times out of 100, these entrepreneurs did not come from a strategic leadership background in which they had years of experience in a managerial role to fully understand all of the intricacies of driving peak performance. This creates a fundamental disconnect when these people then begin running their own business between the leader/employee relationship and how to create the type of relationship that will drive retention and peak performance as well as to become the catalyst for growth in your organization.

If you find yourself in this situation (having launched your business without about a decade of leadership or managerial experience… and getting record-breaking sales growth, profit, and retention out of the people you were leading), don't beat yourself up. Don't become frustrated that you haven't **yet** been able to find, hire, and retain peak performers in your company. Good leadership and management skills are just that – skills. As we covered in the previous chapter, skills can be learned. The key ingredient is motivation and attitude. You need to be motivated to learn leadership and management skills, and those skills are often developed over a period of years and only through experience.

In almost all instances where there is a desire to "fire everyone," including my clients who are running businesses in excess of $20 million/year, the leader/employee relationship is extremely transactional. When you develop a *transactional* relationship with anyone, there is a lack of loyalty, a lack of trust, and a lack of investment that leads to disappointing results. Most of my clients who want to dominate in their fields and really explode their businesses understand that they must be dedicated to becoming a leader who can cultivate extraordinary results… but they're just not sure how. (If you want to see how we help entrepreneurs put a complete A-Z system in place to manage, train, engage, and retain top talent that make you money instead of draining your bank account, go to www.kellyroachcoaching.com/mastermind.)

The constant stress over team is something with which many entrepreneurs struggle. If you're feeling stress about this topic, I assure you, you have a lot of company, and even, a lot of good company. It is a common but solvable problem. The good news is that the reason you always want to fire everyone is because of *you*, and throughout the rest of this book, we'll cover the changes you need to make in order to dissolve the frustrations, challenges, and obstacles that you're currently struggling with when it comes to your team and getting the results you want.

bigger than you.

Warning: Based on the changes you make with what you are about to learn, you may need to make some drastic cultural shifts in the way you run your company, and you may need to make significant changes to your current team in order to implement the steps needed to get the right team behind you.

> *"The big secret in life is that there is no secret. Whatever your goal, you can get there if you are willing to work."*
> ~ Oprah Winfrey

Look Inward

Any time you have ongoing employee issues, struggles, frustrations, or challenges with your team, you must always ask yourself, "What is it about the way I'm leading this team that causes them to fail to invest in the company or that keeps them from wanting to really go above and beyond and do whatever it takes to get the job done?" The answer always lies within you and your approach to leadership. (Yes, this hinges on you making sure the wrong people don't get through the door in the first place.)

Becoming a good leader is a journey in self-development, and it's hard work that the vast majority of business owners aren't willing to do.

In fact, of the very high percentage of businesses that fail, leadership failure is one of the top reasons. You can quickly see that if you're going at it alone or you're working with a duct-taped team (the sort of which we covered in the previous chapter), business owner burnout is extremely high. It's easy to understand why the business owner reaches the point at which they throw up their hands, throw in the towel, and decide they simply cannot do it any longer. This is the very reason thousands of businesses close every year.

> *Set the intention to become an extraordinary leader and you will become one.*

When the business owner is alone or attempting to work with a duct-taped team, they obviously reach a point at which they can no longer sustain the workload or the weight of carrying the organization, and the organization dissolves.

Developing leadership and managerial skills is not a "nice to have." If you want to stay in business for the long term, ultimately with the ability to sell your business for multiples of your current revenue, or if you want to pass your business along as a legacy to support future generations, you must develop solid leadership skills. Again, leadership and management skills are just that – skills... skills that you can learn and sharpen. People who are extraordinary leaders and regularly get record-breaking results from their team are people who work at becoming a better leader every single day. It does not happen by chance and these people are not "born" leaders with an inherent skill set granted to them by genetics.

To repeat: When hiring, you want to hire for motivation and attitude, not skill and knowledge, and the same thing is true for you as the entrepreneur... but ***you***

bigger than you.

must have the right motivation and attitude to develop the leadership skills you need to create an unstoppable dream team and grow your business.

As we covered earlier, a transactional relationship will never yield extraordinary results. Feels obvious, right? However, in our busyness and in our type-A, hyper-focused, fast-moving day, we often don't stop to think about whether or not we're engaging in transactional relationships.

If you want to see a higher investment and more loyal caring team that is willing to go above and beyond to help you achieve your goals – the team you don't want to fire every day – it all begins with changing your own perspective on how this relationship can and should work. It must move from a relationship that is or may be transactional in nature to one that is investment based.

If you view your team members as people to whom you pay an hourly rate to extract a specific result, only thinking about your ROI on that person (i.e., what you're getting from them as a result of what you're paying them), that relationship will be very short lived. It will never have the intangible necessities that will drive extraordinary performance.

On the other hand, when you shift your mindset to investment thinking, you make the choice to become a true mentor to each and every person you bring onto your team. In the beginning of this leader/employee relationship, you are investing multiples more in them than what you are receiving; however, over the lifetime of this relationship, you'll enjoy dividends well beyond your initial investment… even beyond what you could ever fathom.

What do I mean by this? When you initially onboard someone, you need to teach the language, the culture, and the

41

story of your firm. You need to groom them to think like you need and want them to think in order for them to help you achieve your objectives. This takes time. Especially if you're running an online business, the language of the internet, the tools of the trade, and the platforms on which you deliver to your clients are changing daily. As a result, the chance of hiring someone who is already proficient in executing on these various facets is effectively zero. You have two choices when you bring someone into your organization:

1) Invest in them like crazy to get them the best training, tools, and resources to cultivate their ability to develop the strength and talent they need to deliver the results you want… or

2) Take what they're capable of when they join you, simply throwing tasks their way and hope for the best result.

If you picked #2, hope hard… hope really, really hard.

Investment vs. Transaction

Think investment not transactional if you want to develop a winning culture of people who are going to work as hard for your vision as you do.

This also impacts how you teach, train, and delegate tasks. The key frustration that most business owners have when it comes to employees, contractors, or team members is that they throw a smattering of disjointed tactical tasks and have random expectations without ever showing or explaining the how or, more importantly, the why.

The employee must be able to understand why they are doing what they are doing as well as the impact that task has on the organization; otherwise, they can never truly impact your firm in a material way.

This also circles back to developing systems and processes. Either you must have these in place or work with your team to develop them so that tasks are completed correctly but also completed in a way that has both intention and impact on making a difference to the organization and to your bottom line.

You've heard "garbage in/garbage out." The same thinking applies here. If you throw a disorganized mess at your employee, they are going to deliver the same… through no fault of their own. When that happens and you get the urge to fire everyone, it's time to look in the mirror and ask if *you* are the one who deserves to be fired.

> "To add value to others, one must first value others."
> ~ John Maxwell

In the world of sports, when a team of talented players cannot achieve the desired results – aka a winning season – more often than not, the problem lies with the coach. The players can't all be wrong. You can't fire the whole team, but you can fire the coach. When you have the urge to fire your whole team, it's time to take a really hard look at the coach!

If you do not currently have documented systems in place but you are hiring a new person, try out the following steps. This has worked brilliantly for me in the past:

1. Train the person on the step-by-step process for doing each task or objective.
2. Have them take notes as you walk them through documenting in a step-by-step fashion.
3. Have them submit their notes to you to review, make any necessary edits or corrections, and then store this as the official company "process" labeled correctly and easily accessible for future use.

If you have items that are visual in nature, actually do a screen recording and make videos, walking step-by-step through the process. Label and store the recording and… **BOOM**, you are now beginning to document and systematize.

Many times, creating an A to Z checklist for how you want things done within any realm of your business will allow employees to have a tangible form to print and check off as they complete things, and this minimizes the risk of steps being skipped or errors being made.

Simple structural, procedural investments in how you set your employees up for success will make a world of difference in the results they get.

Recap:

> Most entrepreneurs do not come from a background of management or strategic leadership, which is exactly why most of them feel like they want to fire everyone. Hint: get training.
> If you find yourself in the "fire everyone mindset," you must be ready to make drastic changes to your

- organizational culture, the way you are leading, and potentially changes to your existing team.
- Good leadership and management skills are just that – skills. Like any other skill, they can be learned. It is a choice.
- When you have ongoing employee challenges, it's time to look inward and determine what it is you're doing (or not doing) that is driving the outcome.
- Your employees are an investment and if you expect a quick ROI, the relationship will be short lived.
- Again, sound, efficient processes and procedures are a must. If you throw a disorganized mess at an employee, the results you get back will reflect that. Your processes set employees up to succeed or fail.

Action Items:

1. How much time have you previously spent in a leadership or managerial role prior to launching your business? What steps do you need to take to close your knowledge gaps to get better results from your team?

2. If you have employees who have not lived up to your expectations, list some of the ways in which ***you*** have led/managed that have caused their failure. (Be honest!)

3. Think about your relationships with your employees and rate whether they are transactional

or investment based. What changes do you need to get in order to drive the investment you want to receive?

4. How well do your employees understand why they are doing what they are doing? Rank each on a scale of 1-10 (1 = They simply carry out the tasks you give them; 10 = They can clearly describe your vision and how they contribute to it).

To learn how to put everything we discuss in this book into *action* right away, go to www.kellyroachcoaching.com/influence and watch the free, life-changing training now!

Chapter Four:

Reverse the Cycle

I call it the "hire – fire – backslide – burnout" cycle, and unfortunately, I see it a lot with entrepreneurs. If you're a small business owner reading this book, I'm willing to bet that you've experienced the hire – fire – backslide – burnout cycle. This happens when we start to build our teams, and it's also one of the main reasons most small business owners are so resistant to grow their businesses by adding staff. They've had bad hiring and bad "people" experiences. The big problem is that adding staff is the only way to truly grow your business!

Depending on your experience and your skill level as a manager and leader, there can be varying degrees of what I liken to PTSD resulting from the hiring and team-building experiences you may have had. My goal with this book is to allow you to avoid negative staff experiences wherever possible, and my intention with this chapter is to help you understand why it has happened in the past and exactly what you can do to experience the complete opposite in the future.

As I sit and write this, I can assure you that the most enjoyable part of running my own business is the opportunity to work with my team each and every day. There is nothing more rewarding, and there is nothing better for the growth of your business than building a winning team.

However, that only happens through intention, investment, and a whole lot of work establishing processes and systems along the way.

Consider Susan: She was getting very busy and starting to feel stressed and overwhelmed running her business. Her time was tight, and she started to realize that she couldn't do it all herself and needed a helping hand. At the same time, she was running around working on multiple projects with her hands on every aspect of her business. You may be at the very point Susan was, perhaps with one, five, or even 50 different employees all running around, focused only on their own capacity; however, it's all completely disjointed.

> *At some time, almost every entrepreneur goes through the hire-fire-backslide-burnout cycle. Let's make sure this never happens again to you!*

Susan decided that it was, in fact, time to make a hire, but she really did not have time to train anyone. She made a hire and moved quickly through the process because she felt she really needed to relieve the pressure on her, her business, and her family. Things were slipping through the cracks, and she felt she couldn't even come up for air, running as fast and hard as she could, juggling multiple balls and trying to keep them all in the air. While Susan had the best intention to use Tina, her new hire, to relieve the pressure and stress, she still did not have time to train Tina.

She gave Tina a list of tasks and all the things she needed to get off her own plate. In Susan's mind, she thought she was crystal clear about what she needed and how she needed it done. Tina jumped in and started without any real guidance and no day-to-day oversight. Tina had no sense of why her assignments were important or why they needed to

bigger than you.

be done a very specific way. She did not understand the big picture or overall vision for the company. As a brand new employee, Susan effectively gave Tina the autonomy of a manager because she didn't have the time to sufficiently onboard, train, and manage her.

Tina began to fail (through no fault of her own), and Susan's firing process was beginning before the onboarding process was even complete.

Susan received tasks back from Tina, and to her amazement and disappointment, there were countless errors, and she found herself spending more time correcting Tina's work than if she had done it herself in the first place. Susan's frustration was boiling over, and she felt it was time to terminate because she hired Tina to ease the pressure, but the result was that her errors were taking more time out of Susan's day and adding more stress to her life. Susan fell victim to the "easier to do it myself" syndrome, fired Tina, and went back to doing everything herself.

Obviously, Susan made the decision to hire because there was too much work to do herself, and now she was right back in that exact same situation. Enter the backslide part of the cycle: a huge boomerang effect. All the work Susan had pushed off to Tina, came flying back at her… and now it was bigger, heavier, and had more force than the tasks she'd tried to fling to Tina in the first place! Not only did Susan now have all the work back on her plate, she also now had upset clients, invoices that weren't sent, payments that weren't processed, a backload of work, and missed deadlines. It was one hot mess.

Perhaps you've been in the backslide part of the cycle. You can't handle the workload, clients are starting to leave, the morale of your other employees is dropping like a rock.

You have zero time to manage. Any growth you may have experienced before you made the hire has dwindled, and the backslide is gaining negative momentum. Your time is spent correcting tasks, things are slipping through the cracks, balls are being dropped, and revenue and profit are leaking out all over the place.

This brings you, Susan, or any entrepreneur to the final part of the cycle: burnout. It's no surprise that it happens. This final step, entrepreneurial burnout, is one of the leading causes of business failure, right behind a lack of sales and insufficient cash flow. This is the point at which the business owner realizes they simply cannot do it any longer. They give up on their big dream and vision – the whole reason they launched their business in the first place.

They're exhausted; they haven't taken a vacation in years; they feel they've given everything they had to the business and just can't... do... it... another... day.

I've spoken to and learned from eight- and nine-figure entrepreneurs who, in many instances, had the beginnings of serious and permanent health issues, even to the point of requiring hospitalization because of exactly what I just described.

When you consider the stress level, it's no wonder. They failed to approach building their businesses in a strategic and sustainable way.

You Need a New Approach

If you read Susan's story and saw parallels to yourself, please realize you are not alone. This hire – fire – backslide – burnout cycle probably happens to 99 out of every 100 entrepreneurs who reach the $100,000 mark in their businesses.

My expertise is helping these folks build a strategic foundation and sustainable growth trajectory where there are systems in place to allow them to quickly and easily make revenue leaps in the millions because they approached the hiring and team-building process completely differently. We work together for a full year in my Legacy Leaders program to design the exact people plan, infrastructure, systems, and processes you will need to achieve your goals in a simple, sustainable way by building your dream team one small step at a time.

Once Susan understood and embraced the critical importance of having the right infrastructure in place and **took the time to build it**, her subsequent hires enabled her to start building the team she needed to be able to step back from the brink of burnout and grow her business successfully. She's in a much better place today — both financially and mentally — in her business and has broken the hire – fire – backslide – burnout cycle.

The good news for you is that if you've been in the hire – fire – backslide – burnout cycle and you're willing and open to approaching team building and onboarding in whole new way, you, too, can break the cycle (and all its subsequent pains and stresses) and never have to endure it again. You can find the joy my clients and I found in team building and make your hiring process a lucrative one. I've written this book to help you leverage your results through your people. It is possible!

Reverse the Cycle

I shared Susan's example as the wrong way, so now let's talk about the right way because I'm sure you don't want to spend one more second re-living your own similar experience that possibly scarred you for life!

Let's talk about how to have fun in your business and develop raving fans on your team who go on to become incredible ambassadors for your organization and brand... people willing to do anything to help you and your business succeed. Let's also talk about the number one thing that will allow you to grow sustainably year after year after year without compromising your quality of life.

> *If you want to grow, you must have a team. To have an effective team, you must hire well to start.*

The number one thing to consider as an entrepreneur is that you cannot continue to grow without taking on more working hours unless you have leverage! Leverage comes from building a team that runs various aspects of your business without you so that you can scale up without working more hours.

The first step in reversing the cycle is to set your business up in such a way that before you even make your first hire (or another hire), you have things in place that will ensure that your new hire is successful and set up to support you in achieving your goals. You must set up your organization to successfully hire in order to keep your business in business and growing. What do I mean by this? **You must ensure that all elements of your business are**

bigger than you.

documented in systems. This includes sales, marketing, billing, operations, customer support, accounts receivable and payable, etc.

You must get organized first! I have countless clients who come to me for help lessening their sense of overwhelm. It is a leading stressor for entrepreneurs. However, people tend to confuse overwhelm with disorganization. The main reason for overwhelm *is* disorganization. Disorganization is also a main reason that business owners cannot successfully onboard new hires. This disorganization comes from a lack of discipline about documenting what, why, and how everything happens in your business. You must document how you want things done in order for another person to step in and handle the task successfully, ultimately delivering the results you want and need.

Remember John, the brilliant graphic artist I mentioned earlier who struggled every day because he failed to keep accurate time spent on projects and loathed paperwork? He finally understood that he could not continue with the level of

> *A day of focus on organization in your business will pay you dividends for years!*

disorganization he had and that he was on the slippery slope of burnout trying to do it all himself. It was stealing the very creativity he needed to excel at what he produced for his clients.

John finally understood the devastating impact his disorganization had on cash flow and took the time to create a simple but effective timekeeping system — and the discipline to use it. Next, he documented the invoicing process with detailed instructions about how it interfaced with his timesheets so that cost overruns and project scope creep could be captured effectively and invoiced accordingly. With these in place, he found doing the paperwork less loathsome; however, it still required hours of his time.

With this infrastructure created, John could hire an employee to handle this aspect of his business. His employee could step in and accurately invoice for his work, monitor accounts receivable, and keep the cash flowing. Yes, John initially lost some revenue by taking time away from client project work to build his timekeeping system and invoicing infrastructure. However, that lost revenue was quickly made up tenfold when John was now free to concentrate on his core competency. With more hours available for him to produce for clients, revenue continued to grow. Without the burden of the paperwork his disliked so intensely, his attitude improved and with that, his creativity soared. John's success now spiraled upward and in the right direction.

Organization is everything when it comes to building a successful team, and it starts long before your new hire ever walks through the door or logs on to your system. A good action step for you today is to look at your business's key areas of focus and the priorities that support those. Examples:

- Client delivery
- Sales
- Marketing
- Finance, bookkeeping, accounting
- Operations

Use the space below to fill out the three to five key aspects that keep your business running and growing:

bigger than you.

1) _____

2) _____

3) _____

4) _____

5) _____

With this exercise completed, now I want you to take a look at your organizational chart. If you are at the top of that chart and have three to five functions that are essential to your business, do you have a person assigned to each of these key functions?

Do you have a job description created that will allow someone else to successfully carry out these functions? Do you have a documented process for how these functions are to flow and contribute to profit? Is there a step-by-step system that a new hire can sit down and execute on?

It doesn't matter if you're a seasoned entrepreneur with someone already in place handling these functions. You must audit how clean, tight, and clear your systems around the key functions you've list are.

A great starting point with current employees is to do a time audit. Have them record their time, schedule, and tasks. You will be amazed at the wasted time and money on all the wrong things. Usually, this is just a lack of strategic thinking and a misunderstanding of the difference between busy and productive.

If you have a current team but are not happy with their performance, start by doing this audit and really getting clear on where you **want** their hours spent, hour by hour.

Many times, the reason employees are not productive and producing ample profits is that they're just not set up or structured to do so. If you want to increase the productivity and performance of your team, redirect their time, energy, and effort toward things that impact the bottom line.

Train them to think in terms of profit and growth versus tactics and to do's, and your bank account will soar.

If you're just getting started and have not yet made a hire, this is a golden opportunity for you to start off on the right foot. Ask, "What is the first hire I need to make that will allow me to grow faster and more profitably?" Once you answer that question, write a job description that includes both the tasks they need to execute as well as the metrics that will indicate performance and the deliverables that you expect as an outcome of their work. Now you have a clear road map of how this position should function within the organization, and it gives you a list of what you need to document in a clean, organized, functional, and step-by-step process for successful onboarding.

Help your new hire to be clear about what their position entails and how they can implement the process for the right results.

This is the key thing lacking in every business struggling to grow or even be profitable. Owners hire without a job description, without key metrics defined, and without systems that will support the needed execution and accountability to get predictable, repeatable results for both the entrepreneur and the employee.

This is only step one.

bigger than you.

Clear Communication

Before you make a hire, you must set up either yourself or a team member (or some combination) for an onboarding process, so the new hire is walked through the vision and the journey of your business – the "why" behind everything *you* do – who you are in your industry, who you aspire to be, where you want to go as a company and team, and most importantly, the why behind what the new hire does! Then you must back that up with a training plan and onboarding process to teach them how to do it "your way."

When the hire – fire – backslide – burnout cycle happens, it indicates that a strategic onboarding process *or* the day-to-day follow through was lacking or ineffective. There was not a structured, clean training program in which a new hire had clear instructions with bread crumbs listed, so they could backtrack and review and re-learn as needed to deliver the desired outcome. Without this, of course there will be a huge disconnect between your expectations of the new hire and what you get from them… because they never truly understood it in the first place!

In any part of life, whenever there's a disagreement, a dislike, a frustration, or mishap, it is almost always caused by some breakdown in communication. There is no difference in the people management process. When you're frustrated with an employee, contractor, intern, or whomever, there is undoubtedly a breakdown in communication that led to their perspective of "good" and your perspective of "good" being very, very different. The responsibility for this breakdown lies squarely on the business owner's shoulders.

It would be great if new hires could come in and absorb what we want and need through osmosis, but unfortunately, that's impossible (as of now; please let me know if you figure this out before I do...☺). You must demonstrate what good looks like, give them a step-by-step process, and itemize clear and specific expectations, so they know exactly whether or not what they're doing is delivering the right results. Without this clarity, you have no right to be frustrated, disappointed, or upset with anyone you hire.

So why doesn't proper onboarding and training happen? The most common reason I hear and the challenge for most entrepreneurs: time. Specifically, not enough of it. Let me suggest that it's not that isn't **enough** time; it's that business owner does not understand the importance of spending their time here. What I can guarantee you is that there is literally nothing more important.

> *So many problems can be avoided and issues overcome with a little more effort in your communication.*

What most business owners or hiring managers in general don't realize is that the pace you set from day one shapes the employee's perception of what you expect from them. The way you structure and organize their day – with precision or sloppiness – lets them know how seriously to take how they manage their time. Accountability from day one, starting with homework, self-study and independent learning, determines whether they see their role as a clock-in/clock-out situation or an in-it-to-win-it/do-whatever-it-takes type culture. All of this is set from day one. The way someone is introduced to your organization literally determines the productivity and profits they will generate on your behalf for months, maybe years into the future.

bigger than you.

As my experienced leaders all know and have experienced, it is far harder to correct bad habits and fix poor performance than it is to do it the right way the first time, no matter how painful it might be to slow down long enough to do this.

What I most want you to realize in reading this book is that you can work less and earn more (in a range of millions!) in your business by learning how to create effective roles within your organization, onboarding your staff effectively, and then leveraging them to get a positive ROI. There is no limit to your growth without impacting your working hours if you understand and embrace this process.

No doubt you believe that making money and keeping your sanity is an important part of being in business for yourself! Having an effective team is the key.

Ongoing Training

Now that you have an employee onboarded with a well-defined and documented job description and processes, and you have clearly communicated your expectations, a training program is the next step. When I say "training program," I don't want you to think this only applies to major corporations or multi-million-dollar entities. It doesn't matter if you have one employee or tens of thousands. Every organization can and should have a training program for new employees.

> *"Successful leaders see the opportunities in every difficulty rather than the difficulty in every opportunity."*
> *~ Reed Markham*

A program may be as simple as them sitting with you for the first 30 minutes each day for the first 30 days or intermittently sitting with a manager, mentor, or current employee who is already performing at expectation. There is no right or wrong... except for not having one at all. Regardless, there must be a structured pathway to get them from the stage of not knowing anything about your company to becoming culturally integrated, so they can be a valuable asset to your company.

In addition to training, there is also the day-to-day management of the employee. A big frustration I hear from managers a lot is a huge disappointment in the employee's mindset... or lack thereof. For small business owners especially, it can be very discouraging when their employees have a tactic driven versus profit driven mindset. But this, again, is a learned skillset and mindset.

When we focus on managing employees to tactical tasks and to do's, they become masters at marking things off the list versus strategically innovating for growth. If you want to cultivate a different way of thinking in your team, it starts with investing in teaching them a new way of thinking and then managing to that.

As the business owner reading this book, you must understand that every seat in your company needs to be filled by a strategic partner.

That doesn't mean that every employee is guiding and directing the future of your company. It means that every seat is a profit center. If there is a seat that is not profitable, then it is either

    a) coming directly out of your own income
       or

b) creating undue and most times unsustainable pressure on the other employees.

For most entrepreneurs, this is exactly what happens: employees are not profitable. Entrepreneurs and business owners are actually paying to have employees because unprofitable employees' salaries come out of the business owner's pocket.

If you start with a plan and map to get each new hire profitable and you have a clear roadmap to get them there even before they start, you are well on your way to creating a high-performance culture and reversing this cycle for good!

Once you've onboarded an employee and they fully understand how to handle their role with a high level of excellence, it's time to invest in the employee's growth and development, so they can make a bigger, more profitable impact on your company and enable growth even further.

In my Legacy Leaders program, we focus on the daily investment needed in the relationship with every employee to help them become an impact player.

An impact player is someone who makes their role profitable and contributes to the forward movement of the organization rather than simply working to maintain the status quo.

This occurs through weekly one-on-one time during which you focus on employee's performance, growth, and what they can do to achieve next-level results. It includes providing training on new tools, resources, and strategies to do their jobs more efficiently and with more impact. Additionally, it includes placing them in mentorship relationships (either with you or someone else in your company or outside of it) to help ***them*** grow.

Small business owners tend to be very resistant to manage people and hold them accountable in daily tasks. Many of them perceive a negative stigma around it. However, coaching your staff is making an investment in them. Let me repeat that because it's so important: **Coaching your staff is making an investment in them!** This investment can be more valuable to the employee in the long term than the salary you pay them.

Investing in Your Assets

If you want to hire people who are going to stay with your firm for the long haul and become impact players, putting money on the bottom line consistently for you, it makes sense that you have to nurture that. It's like a plant. The plant needs sunshine and water to grow; otherwise, it withers and dies. The analogy with employees is the same. When most employees leave a company, they are actually leaving the manager because there is no longer investment in them (or so they feel). They move on to another organization where that investment exists and they have more opportunity for their own growth (or so they think).

> *The degree to which you invest in your team is the degree to which they'll invest in your company.*

Don't ever think that you can't win the best talent because you can't pay as much. There are many other facets of employment that people value as much or even more than salary: mentorship, growth, education, opportunity to try new things, etc. Feeling appreciated also leads the list of what employees are looking for in a career in which they are willing to invest and commit to over the long term.

For a cheat sheet on how to put together the "attractor factor employment package" for your firm to get the best talent coming to you even if you're not the highest paying business on the block, go to: www.kellyroachcoaching.com/attractorfactor.

I want you to think about the employee expenses that you incur in your business. They are assets. For every day that you fail to invest in those assets, they deteriorate. Every day, the people investments in your firm are either growing – becoming more invested, or they're deteriorating – going backward and disengaging, even a little bit. The latter ultimately leads to their departure from your company.

When an employee quits or leaves for a better opportunity, as business owners, we're typically shocked and disappointed. However, when you look back over the history of their tenure, it's obvious why they made the decision they did: They were not feeling appreciated, they were not being invested in, and they were not recognized and rewarded appropriately. These failures happen day by day and continue to accumulate over time. It is ***rarely*** one big issue or occurrence that leads to the departure. Instead, it's always "the straw that broke the camel's back."

In our busyness, it's easy to shed the mantle of responsibility. We convince ourselves that it is not our fault, so we allow ourselves to think the surprise and shock we feel is warranted. Again, a departure rarely, if ever, comes out of nowhere. It is a series of hundreds of small decisions that you, as the owner and manager, made (or didn't make) each day that leads the employee to believe that they would be better off heading for the door, logging off, and working elsewhere.

> *"I've learned that people will forget what you said, people will forget what you did, but people will never forget how you made them feel." ~ Maya Angelou*

If you can capture this one mindset – that of investing in your employees and remembering that it's the daily little things that will make a positive or negative difference and impact the employees' desire to become profitable, impact players – then you can reverse the hire – fire – backslide – burnout cycle and stop the human resources revolving door. Invest in your team, no matter how big or small it is, each and every day, so they'll make a higher-level investment in you. This directly translates to the growth and profitability of your company.

Recap:

> ➤ It is imperative to go through the essentials checklist for new hire preparation before you get

> someone started to prevent and eliminate this cycle. This includes the job description, KPIs, a system for accountability, and the training and onboarding plan.
> ➤ To break the cycle, you must slow down and focus first on organization, then on documentation.
> ➤ Define your most critical functions and have someone on your organizational chart responsible for them, with job descriptions and key metrics clearly defined and documented.
> ➤ Whenever there's a disagreement, a dislike, a frustration, or mishap, it is almost always caused by some breakdown in communication. As the business owner, you are responsible for clear communication.
> ➤ After successful onboarding, employee training must be ongoing, so they can continue to grow and become impact players for your organization.
> ➤ You must invest in your human assets. The degree to which you invest in them is the degree to which they'll deliver the results you want and become ambassadors for your organization.

Action Items:

1. Rate how similar you are to Susan on a scale of 1-10 (1 = I thought you wrote that story about me; 10 = I can't believe anyone approaches team building like that).

2. Document everything a new employee needs to know about the history of your company, your place in the

industry, your vision for what you want to achieve, etc.

3. Be sure you completed the exercise about defining the key aspects that keep your business running and growing and who might fill those roles and the systems you've built around them.

4. If you haven't hired yet, ask and answer: "What is the first hire I need to make that will allow me to grow faster and more profitably?"

5. Take some time to think about recent errors, misunderstandings, disagreements, and frustrations and jot down how a lack of communication was at the core of each one.

6. List three ways in which you can interact with every employee on a weekly basis to continue your investment in them.

To learn how to put everything we discuss in this book into *action* right away, go to
www.kellyroachcoaching.com/influence
and watch the free, life-changing training now!

Chapter Five:

Still Broke?

Are you still broke but you're running a million-dollar business? If so, you aren't alone. If you haven't reached that level yet in your business and think it's impossible to be broke running a business that has that sort of revenue, think again. I assure you there are countless businesses that on the surface may appear to be successful based on revenue; however, there is a ton of debt with the business owner taking no less than an entry-level salary! If you find yourself in that situation, I want to help you correct it. If you aren't there, I want to help you avoid it.

This is an important piece of the entire leadership puzzle. Perspective on where your expenses are going and how you are managing them is everything. Recall for a moment that in the previous chapter, we covered the concept that every seat in your business must be turning a profit. Any seat that is failing to do so is coming right out of your pocket.

Most entrepreneurs start out with the idea that they must reinvest as much of the revenue as possible into the business in the first few years to be able to grow to the desired level. At the early stage, many entrepreneurs invest 100 percent or even greater than 100 percent (taking on personal debt) of the revenue in order to grow. As a coach, I can look at a company's P&L and quickly and very accurately predict where things are going to become problematic (if they haven't reached that stage already) and what needs to change in order to get on the path to profitability… with the entrepreneur putting more money in their personal bank account.

As I said, in most instances, the business owner – with good intentions – is reinvesting all or almost all back into the company. As the business grows, they may take only a menial salary in contrast to the overall revenue they're taking in. The result: They're broke. This is a dangerous strategy, and you have to walk a very fine line. On one hand, you do need to reinvest in your business, especially in the early stages, if you want to grow and succeed over the long term. However, the misappropriation of funds is one of the key things that takes entrepreneurs down and knocks them out of the game.

> *Successful entrepreneurs spend money wisely rather than on ego boosters.*

Because of the hire – fire – backslide – burnout cycle, business owners resolve to attempt to grow their businesses in ways other than investing in their team. This leads to them spending on things like equipment, space in which to work, tools, technology, and all sorts of things that are nice to have but do not catapult the business forward in terms of growth.

Look at your own spending. I bet you'll come up with hundreds of things that you've stupidly spent money on (that now you wish you hadn't) that provided no true ROI in growing your business.

The key differentiator between the entrepreneurs who thrive and those barely surviving is where and how they spend their money. Those thriving are spending on growth-oriented things that allow the business to generate more

bigger than you.

leads, close more clients, and serve a bigger population. This includes things like staff, advertising and marketing, and product development.

Look at the expenses in your business today. Stop reading for a moment and take a look at last month's expenses. Separate the expenses into two categories: maintenance and growth expenses. Growth expenses are the things you spend money on that will bring you a return in greater revenue and profit. For example, an employee who is generating sales is a growth expense (expense being their salary and benefits). You pay them X-amount per month and get back some increase over X. The same is true of advertising and marketing expenses. Done correctly, these generate an increase in business.

On the other hand, maintenance expenses are recurring expenses that keep you right where you are and maintaining the status quo. These expenses really don't move your business forward and have no intrinsic value in terms of bottom-line results. Consider things like space (unless you are a manufacturer or distributor), fancy furniture, tech tools, a big office, and décor. Print advertising can fall into this category unless you are truly getting results from it (most are not these days). You may get an ego boost seeing a printed ad for your business, but are your prospects also seeing it and acting on it? These expenses include money going out on things that are non-essential (or that you'll realize are non-essential by the time you finish the book!) and fail to generate a positive return in terms of more clients or greater profit.

Consider a few growth/maintenance differentiating factors in seemingly similar expenses: If you purchase a new computer system because the old one is worn out and replace it with the same, that's a maintenance expense. However, if you purchase a new system that enables you to expand capacity and serve greater numbers of clients, that would be considered a growth expense. If you have a trucking company and replace a truck, that's maintenance. Add a truck and that's growth. If you replace a piece of equipment in your business that will allow your staff to work faster and produce more, that is a growth expense. However, what usually happens is that you invest in that new thing, get it, don't maximize it correctly, and now you've spent the money but are not getting any true added value... which equals money lost just to maintain it.

> *"Rule #1: Never lose money. Rule #2: Never forget Rule #1."*
> *~ Warren Buffett*

Once you've reviewed these two categories of expenses, you want to shift as much as possible into things that are going to enable growth. Make sure your money is spent on things that will also help you become a better leader and a more effective CEO; that will help your team better serve your clients so they'll stay longer, spend more, and refer more business; and that will help you expand better quality leads, so you can ultimately drive more profitable revenue.

Too many entrepreneurs are spending loads and loads of money on all sorts of things that keep them marking time rather than moving forward and growing their businesses. They have too many expenses that do not tie back into the bottom line. This is exactly why there can be businesses with a million dollars in revenue with owners who are broke and with massive amounts of debt.

bigger than you.

Proper Allocation

The first step is to be honest with yoursel[f] exercise I just suggested. If you skipped over it, you [need to go] back and complete this if you want to grow your company and improve your own income. Are you actually spending any money in order to grow? Are you consciously making an investment to grow each month? Do you have any entries in the growth category of your expenses… or are they all falling into the maintenance category?

I get entrepreneurs who come to me who aren't spending money on their team, aren't spending on advertising, aren't spending anything in growth categories and then wonder why they're stuck… wonder why they're still broke! It's very black and white. If you want an investment to bring a return, you have to invest in the first place.

Secondly, get very aggressive in cutting your maintenance expenses – the things on which you're spending that are not generating an increase in revenue or profit for you. Cut the things that are "ego-driven" – those things that look nice on paper and may make you feel better but are not contributing anything to the bottom line. Eliminate the non-essentials that are not driving profitable growth. Finally, re-allocate these funds into things that can actually grow your business.

It Ties Back to Your Team

Proper allocation doesn't stop with your expenses. Each and every member of your team must be treated as a profit center. You must get a return on your investment (the salary and benefits you pay) for having that person on payroll in your business. This is one of the biggest hurdles with which I see entrepreneurs in my Legacy Leadership program struggle. For example, an accounting person can help save you thousands. A customer support person can be generating new referrals. A salesperson must be managed and held accountable for a specific sales goal every week. Every role in your organization must deliver something to the bottom line and a net positive ROI.

As business owners, we often don't take responsibility for setting up our staff so that their job descriptions and how and where they focus their time and energy are allocated to the things that can produce profit. Apply common sense here: If you're hiring without structuring the role so it provides net bottom-line benefit, you are paying for their salary out of your own pocket – the money that should be going to your own family! (No doubt your spouse would not be happy to read this part.)

> *Everyone on your team is a profit center!*

So what's the solution? Keeping in mind what we covered previously, be sure you build your job descriptions for every role by first answering **how** this employee will provide growth and a net benefit.

Think it's not possible? So did my Legacy Leaders program members before we went through and structured every role in their companies to make them money. Yes, it's a new language; yes, it takes some energy and effort to learn, but most importantly, this can and will work for your business if you let it!

How are we going to yield a positive ROI? What will this person do on a daily basis that results in profitable

bigger than you.

growth? It starts with you, and it ends with y(
you in where you have the employee invest (
energy, and it ends with you in terms of how
them and hold them accountable to deliver on the
you outlined to start.

Your employee can only serve your firm to the
that you've set them up to succeed. Where you point their focus is exactly where their energy will flow. What you establish as your expectation is what your employee is going to understand as their responsibility.

As I said already, it begins and ends with you. You have so much more control than you realize to leverage massive amounts of growth by re-directing your employees' time toward the things that will actually make money for the company rather than simply having people completing tactical tasks and to-do's.

You have all the power in the world, and it comes down to focus, taking action, and putting your energy into the things that are going to help you and everyone who's supporting you to get a return for growth.

Recap:

> - It is entirely possible for the owner of a business with a million dollars in revenue to only be earning an entry-level salary themselves.
> - There is a fine line to walk between investing revenues for growth and taking an adequate salary – strike a balance.
> - The key differentiator between entrepreneurs who are thriving and those who are struggling lies in how and where money is spent.

- You must understand the difference between a growth and a maintenance expense and re-allocate as much as possible into the growth category.
- Every employee is a profit center, so everything they do should be contributing to your bottom line. Failure to make this happen means their salary is coming out of your pocket.
- Write every job description by asking, "How will this role support our mission, vision and goals?" and this includes getting and staying profitable.
- It always starts and ends with you!

Action Items:

1. Have you set targets in terms of % expenses, % income, % taxes, etc. for how money is allocated in your business? If not, start now.

2. Make a chart with "Growth" in one column and "Maintenance" in another and list every expense you had last month in the appropriate column.

3. Determine which maintenance expenses can be eliminated or converted to growth expenses and plan how you can make that happen.

4. List your employees and their salaries and cost of benefits and overall expenses given resources, tools, training required to support them and their role.

bigger than you.

5. Look at that list and itemize what they do and determine if/how their tasks contribute to profitability and growth. If they're not contributing to profit, look at how you would need to re-work their focus to go from expense to income earning in your business.

6. Eliminate the tasks of each employee that do not contribute to your profit and growth or redefine them so that they do.

To learn how to put everything we discuss in this book into *action* right away, go to
www.kellyroachcoaching.com/influence
and watch the free, life-changing training now!

Still Broke?

Chapter Six:

Remove the #1 Bottleneck to Growth

When you launched your business and signed on as an entrepreneur, you signed up to work for the craziest boss on the planet – you.

You have total control over your own success (or failure) as a business owner. Sometimes, you as your own boss can be the most fantastic thing in the world; however, it can also be very difficult because it's the only position you can have in your career in which you have no one overseeing what you're doing. You have no one providing feedback, helping you course correct when needed, and most importantly, calling you out on your excuses and other "b.s." that comes out of your mouth.

Every entrepreneur in every industry and, in fact, anyone who has made it to the highest levels (e.g., Olympic athletes, musicians, politicians, entrepreneurs, etc.) all have one thing in common – they seek outside counsel, coaching, and mentorship in some form or facet.

This counsel often comes at great expense, but these top performers fully understand the positive impact it generates. It provides a "voice of reason," a collaborative partner, and strategic advisor.

It's important for you to understand that your business can only succeed to the degree that *you* grow, both personally and professionally. Ultimately, every bottleneck in your business and the cap on your growth always comes back to you.

Only when you adopt and embrace this position and mindset of full responsibility can you truly become extraordinary in your field. This recognition – your responsibility for your own success or failure – is the key to undoing the bottlenecks that are holding you back!

You might want to blame outside forces: "It's this process; it's this machine or piece of equipment or software; it's this person; it's the industry; it's the clients; it's this 'thing' that is out of my control that is the bottleneck." The reality? There is a solution to every problem and an alternate perspective on overcoming, working around, or conquering any and every obstacle.

When a problem persists in your business, it comes back to you. It indicates that you haven't yet stepped up to the plate as the leader in your organization to address the poor performance, to break the industry norm, or innovate your way through to a solution. Very simply, it always comes back to you.

Business owners can get caught up in many things that keep them as the bottleneck to growth. One of the biggest reasons we get stuck and frozen in place is the need for control, driven by our fear of letting go. This is also the reason many entrepreneurs don't hire and work on building an unstoppable team in the first place. Their excuse is that they can't find anyone who's competent to do the work or anyone who can perform the work as well as them or to their standards. This is completely false. This misconception is the very thing causing a bottleneck.

Once again (and as we covered earlier), it comes down to simplification versus complexity. The difficulty in onboarding someone in your organization is a bottleneck to growth. If it's very difficult for someone to execute on the standards you've created and the process is not replicable, you've created your own barrier to growth because you've made it impossible to scale. Your job is to systematize, create processes, and engineer simplicity and ease throughout your entire business. Doing so allows someone else to step in, learn appropriately, and execute at least part of or even your entire system.

> *"Fools ignore complexity. Pragmatists suffer it. Some can avoid it. Geniuses remove it."*
> *~ Alan Perlis*

Here is something else to consider: How have you structured the workload? Many entrepreneurs start from the point of doing it all and being it all, and that's what they attempt to transition to an employee. This creates an unmanageable workload as well as a scattered, disjointed, disorganized approach to the entire organization. Again, this is unscalable and unreplicable… a bottleneck. Take a step back and determine if your inability to find or keep an employee who isn't working to your standards is because the standards are unrealistic. I don't mean that they are too high; I mean that they are too complicated. This is a prime reason employees and business owners alike get burned out.

Slow down and give this careful consideration if you want to be able to step back from the day-to-day operations and instead lead and manage at a higher level. Without doing so, you'll never find a team who can run your organization and enable sustainable, healthy growth that lets your company stand the test of time.

Replicate McDonald's

Take time to revisit each piece of each process and ask if it makes sense for one employee to handle every step…

or in fact, is every step even needed? Perhaps you've struggled to find someone to do a particular job because it has become overly and unnecessarily complex. Look again to see if any or every process can be broken down into smaller phases or steps that can then be divided into different roles for different team members, allowing you to better balance the workload. Also consider whether the process or task has entire pieces that can simply be removed. So often, when I am working with entrepreneurs to help them grow faster, it comes down to simplifying and clarifying and then spending time on the right things while letting go of the wrong ones. It's not that you or your team needs to do more and work harder; it's that you need to simplify more and focus on the things that matter. (Yes, easier said than done, but it's essential!)

After doing this, take another look at your job descriptions to refine those to make them easier to "plug and play."

McDonald's is a great example of this. Every single job, every task, every minute detail is pared down to the second in terms of how long a process should take, in addition to clearly defining what to do and how to do it with exact precision.

The result? Complete consistency (a lynchpin to their worldwide success) and scalability! Think about how many franchisees buy into the system to replicate the corporate success and then how many new hires each of those franchisees has to make. It's astronomical. As an entry-level job, there is regular and anticipated turnover, yet locations continue to be successful and the experience from location to location is similar and replicable. Employees can be onboarded and trained according to established and time-tested procedures.

Most entrepreneurs take exactly the opposite approach – they build an organization that is exotically rare with more exceptions than rules, and that is difficult if not impossible to infiltrate. The result is that they've created a giant bottleneck to growth.

No one can step in to help, so the entrepreneur *is* the number one bottleneck to growth. If you've created a high level of complexity with barriers around you, others will never be able to help you and they will never meet your standards. They can't help you help yourself. All bottlenecks ultimately stem from this point.

I've already mentioned the importance of systematizing and organizing every process in your company. Failure to do so is one of the biggest hurdles to unlocking the bottlenecks and freeing the logjams that occur with workflow. When you take the time – and really take all the time you need – to systematize and organize, I assure you, your systems open up for exponential growth forever.

"Why" to the Third Degree

One of the best ways to alleviate bottlenecks is to track them back to their point of origin, just like tracking a logjam back upstream.

Case Study: Sandra's manufacturing company was having a cash flow problem. It was a huge issue for Sandra, the owner, who was losing sleep every night and obsessing when the mail arrived every day, worried about how many checks might arrive and what that day's bank deposit would be. "Will I have to tap the credit line just to make payroll?" All employees noticed the stress level, and those with knowledge of the financials were aware of the cash flow issue. Morale was dropping;

employees were starting to stress about their own job security. "Are we going to have to shut down?"

When we looked at it closely, it turned out that it was really a bottleneck issue more than anything else. It was not an issue with quality, lead conversion, sales, or customer service. When we tracked the problem back upstream and repeatedly asked "Why," the solution started to reveal itself. Here's what it looked like:

Why #1: *Why aren't checks arriving, creating a cash flow problem? Because invoices aren't being sent out consistently and on time.*

Why #2: *Why aren't invoices being sent out consistently and on time? Because Chris is in charge of invoicing and often doesn't get enough information to bill properly and has to go back to the sales rep for clarification. There is always a delay in getting that information since sales reps are usually on the road.*

Why #3: *Why don't sales reps provide consistent information for invoicing? Because there isn't a system in place to define for them exactly what they have to provide to Chris to create an accurate and timely invoice.*

In examining this particular bottleneck, we suggested that Sandra develop a system and a form for sales reps to submit to Chris for invoicing. All considerations from each particular job and for each particular client were spelled out and documented on the form. There was also a deadline instituted for these forms to be submitted to Chris. Sales reps now knew exactly what had to be reported and by when. As a result, invoices started going out on a regular basis, and Chris could actually do that part of the job faster because everything was submitted in black and white. A month after the form was developed and the process refined, checks started to flow in regularly, and cash flow improved. Morale picked up, and Sandra was able to begin focusing on strategic growth initiatives versus scrambling day to day to prevent overdrafts in the company accounts. Team members were happy, no longer worried

bigger than you.

about job security, and were able to focus on doing their jobs to the best of their ability.

Within a matter of months, Sandra, went from fearing she would go bankrupt and lose the business altogether to net positive with consistent month-over-month growth. The system not only corrected the cash flow problem but skyrocketed morale and allowed everyone to refocus on generating and closing new business so the company could grow.

Sandra's story is an example of Legacy Leadership at work. So the question I have for you is: How close could your next breakthrough worth hundreds of thousands (if not millions) in your business be if you really got serious about eliminating the bottlenecks and systematizing your team's success?

I encourage you to ask "Why" at least three times to every bottleneck, and you will almost always see a new or better solution.

Here's an exercise that will help you break up the logjams in your business and keep work, revenue, and profit flowing smoother. Consider your five biggest bottlenecks in your organization. Perhaps like Sandra, one might be cash flow. List those challenges along with the negative impact they are having on your company, your employees, or you, then ask "Why" at least three times to determine what steps you can take that you haven't tried before.

Bottleneck #1:	Negative Impact:
Why #1:	
Why #2:	
Why #3:	
Possible Solution:	

Bottleneck #2:	Negative Impact:
Why #1:	
Why #2:	
Why #3:	
Possible Solution:	
Bottleneck #3:	**Negative Impact:**
Why #1:	
Why #2:	
Why #3:	
Possible Solution:	
Bottleneck #4:	**Negative Impact:**
Why #1:	
Why #2:	
Why #3:	
Possible Solution:	
Bottleneck #5:	**Negative Impact:**
Why #1:	
Why #2:	
Why #3:	
Possible Solution:	

bigger than you.

The bottom line is for you to determine what you can do or try to solve each of these bottlenecks. Honestly, when you peel back every bottleneck and ask "Why" at least three times (perhaps some problems will require continuing that exercise and continuing to ask "Why" five, six, seven or more times), you will always arrive at the core issue that is causing the logjam. Moreover, you will discover that every struggle you face always comes back to a solution to which you have not yet committed!

> *"In most organizations, the bottleneck is at the top of the bottle." ~ Peter Drucker*

After reading through the case study (perhaps it's similar or identical to an issue you face) and going through the exercise of identifying your bottlenecks and asking the series of "Whys" that you need to, you'll see that there is a solution to every problem in business. It may not be the first one that comes to mind or that you try, it may not be the easiest one, and it may not be the one that you like, but there is a way to get over every hurdle you face.

If you apply the "Why" exercise to every problem, take full ownership of it, and are really honest about what steps are needed to arrive at the solution you want, you'll realize that you are responsible for why the issue has been occurring. Moreover, you are the one who can and must make the decisions required to change things for the better.

This level of control in your business is an unbelievable gift… and it can also be a curse. This is exactly why I began this chapter sharing the idea that no Olympian ever made it to the medal podium without a coach. It is very difficult when you are in the day-to-day operations, way down in the weeds of the tactics dealing with clients and employees, working through all of the things that need to be handled to see clearly and make proactive decisions that will break the bottleneck. It's often a case of "not being able to see the forest for the trees"!

Find a way to slow down (very difficult when you are in the throes of trying to solve one crisis after another) and take the time to put in place the steps and processes required to create a permanent solution instead of a temporary Band-Aid. When business owners lack the discipline to slow down and create permanent solutions rather than employing one temporary fix after another (that pile on one another, leading to crazy complexity), problems persist, grow, and ultimately take the business down.

Temporary fixes never allow you to address the root problem, so that problem manifests in continuing worse ways!

Sometimes when business owners come to me with problems, the solutions seem so simple and obvious that I start to second-guess myself. I start asking myself, "Wait… what am I missing here?" I repeat my understanding to them regarding their issue to ensure I am really capturing their problem. Ninety-nine percent of the time, the solution is that simple and obvious but they just can't see it.

This is why we all need outside counsel, myself included. I realize that when I'm "in it," it's really hard to see what may be an obvious solution, which is why I have

bigger than you.

invested hundreds of thousands of dollars in outside counsel, training, and development personally and will continue to do so for the duration of my career.

You've heard the phrase "the simplest solution is typically the best one," and it's absolutely true!

Primary Problems

Almost every problem in your business (and every bottleneck to growth caused by the problem) is caused by one of three things: people, profit, or processes.

1. **"People"** could mean that you don't have enough people, don't have the right people, or that you have people who are not being managed correctly to allow you to achieve the ROI needed to maintain your profitability and achieve your goals and the growth you want.
2. **"Profit"** includes pricing confidence and positioning, effective sales and marketing, and the systems around how you grow your business. Even with all of the resources and information that is available, the lack of profitable sales is the number one issue that causes businesses to fail. According to Statistic Brain, the failure rate of all U.S. companies after five years was over 50 percent and over 70 percent by the 10-year mark. (as quoted in *Entrepreneur.com*, "Why Some Startups Success (and Why Most Fail), Feb. 81, 2017").
3. **"Processes"** mean having the correct infrastructure, systems in place, and ***documented*** procedures that are followed

with precision and excellence in the way you run your business every single day.

All problems stem from these things, and yes, there are complexities and "run offs"; however, when you examine any problem and put it through the "Why" exercise, you will invariably discover that it comes back to one of these three things. At the very center of all of this is building a winning team. There is no one person who can do it all in order to keep a business not only running but enjoying sustainable growth.

> *"Alone we can do so little, together we can do so much."* ~ Helen Keller

Think about all of the talent, skill, and roles that are needed to run a business. There are so many different personalities, perspectives, and skill sets needed for success. If you have one person fulfilling multiple roles, the majority of them will not be done very well – and this includes you, if you are trying to do them yourself. Rather, as the business owner, you must embrace your responsibility to build a winning team. Each role needed to grow your company should be filled by a person who is not only completely capable of the tasks needed but has the passion, drive, and integrity to do them at a world-class level (eventually). Your team members should be fanatical about precision and excellence, and you have the ability to create a culture that drives people to want to do so.

How You Handle Sales

This brings us back to the bottleneck that surrounds generating enough profitable sales to keep your business not only afloat but growing. When you continue to delve into this problem, you'll find it brings you back to people. I actually find it fascinating that, although the traditional approach and tried-and-true method of business success is through outside sales, many (but not all) entrepreneurs place hiring an outside sales person **last** on their list.

> *No one person has the expertise and skill set to handle every role in any business. Teams are critical.*

Most entrepreneurs turn up their noses at the idea of sales or the traditional "outside" sales model to grow their businesses because the online world has spun the idea of quick fame and fast money online so out of control that most people getting into business today don't even consider the need for a sales team.

Interestingly enough, besides the one-in-a-million tech company or app that gets funding or a big investor behind it, the vast majority of **all** million- and billion-dollar companies got there through building a rock solid outside sales team. Think about it: A solid outside sales team makes perfect sense if you want to grow fast, close enormous amounts of clients fast, and achieve industry leadership... right?

I will never forget interviewing the head of outside sales for Facebook on my podcast, *Unstoppable Success Radio*. I use this as an example because (although social selling is straight up amazing and a personal favorite of mine), don't you think if any company out there would have the tools, technology, and resources to eliminate outside sales, Facebook would? Right. Yet, they continue to use outside sales... because it works! Don't follow the sheep and go right over the cliff.

Unfortunately, for most entrepreneurs today, hiring a sales team is not even a consideration in their business model. It's a head-scratcher because clearly there is no business if there are no sales and profit. I find that when businesses are struggling to grow, it is not because the sales team is underperforming... it is usually because the sales team doesn't even exist in the first place!

On the other hand, when I find a struggling business that does, in fact, have a sales team, I also uncover that the sales team is not being managed effectively or given the support and structure they need to achieve the growth expectations of the business owner (and more to come on this in a later chapter).

I want you to end this chapter with the clear understanding that you can achieve the most unbelievable, fabulous, exponential, practically immeasurable growth in your business, and the first step in clearing the hurdles that stand in the way of this type of growth is taking total ownership. You must understand that you have to slow down and identify each of the bottlenecks to growth. Then you must step up and lead by making the right decisions that will address the root causes of the bottlenecks, so they can be undone, allowing you to tap into incredible growth. You have all the power in the world.

Once you go through this process and apply the exercise in this chapter with every new problem that arises in your company as you grow, you'll quickly see that taking the time to uncover and address the root cause will create big positive changes in your organization… and you'll never look back.

You'll wonder why you waited so long, letting pain and frustration fester. You'll wonder why you allowed that weight on your own shoulders for so long. I'm certain this will then motivate you to always take the time in the future to examine bottlenecks and make the right decisions to break them rather than apply quick but temporary solutions that only further complicate your business.

I believe you will also begin to trust the wisdom of seeking outside counsel to help you see the bigger picture (the forest rather than the trees) and to get the support, feedback, guidance, and most importantly the accountability needed to help you truly step up as a leader to make the right investments, solve the right problems, and put the right things in place that will explode your growth.

Recap:

- Being the boss is a blessing and a curse. You have total control, but unless you seek outside counsel, you don't have anyone holding you accountable and can sometimes completely miss what's right in front of you as a solution.
- Business owners often create bottlenecks because they fear hiring employees to create the team they

really need in order to grow. Stretch that courage muscle!
- The workload structure is often another bottleneck creator. If someone can't work to your standards, it is because your standards are too complicated. How can you help simplify the process so your team can and will succeed?
- Remember that McDonald's has tens of thousands of new hires every year who are successfully onboarded because the organization has meticulously detailed every task with the result being complete consistency and scalability. Simplicity = Scalability.
- Use the "Why" exercise on every problem. Asking "Why" at least three times typically brings you to the root cause and ultimate solution.
- Problems always come back to people, profit, or processes.
- The most successful companies have dedicated sales reps. It's counterintuitive to believe you can grow your business without a sales strategy. No sales, no business. Are you going about it the hard way?

Action Items:

1. Take a look at your processes. First, are they documented? As we covered in Chapter 1, if they are not, you must make this a priority. If you have documentation, review each and every step of every process to determine how and where you can simplify it and break it into

smaller pieces to balance the workload. Keep the McDonald's approach in mind as you're working on this.

2. Be certain to complete the exercise in which you determine your five biggest bottlenecks (you likely have more than five, so start with the five biggest) and apply the "Why" test. Implement the solutions you uncover.

3. Think about the problems to which you've applied a Band-Aid rather than taking the time to figure out and implement a ***permanent*** solution. Failure to do so will keep you continually trying to solve the same problem (or its offshoot) repeatedly.

4. If you do not have an outside sales rep, reconsider this as a solution to powerful, sustainable growth.

5. Consider working with a coach for the beneficial feedback, support, and accountability they can offer.

To learn how to put everything we discuss in this book into ***action*** right away, go to
www.kellyroachcoaching.com/influence
and watch the free, life-changing training now!

Remove the #1 Bottleneck to Growth

Chapter Seven:

Step Up and Lead... or Die

I would say you have to step up and lead or your business may die; however, in reality, without effective leadership, your business probably **will** die.

When we look at the huge percentage of businesses that fail (and even those that are squeaking by with the owner taking what amounts to little more than entry-level salary... or less), the number one cause to point to is sales.

It's almost always at the heart of every business failure, which is why I continually stress the need for a systematic approach to sales and encourage entrepreneurs to have a fanatical approach to this particular process.

A strong process for sales and marketing, especially in the digital age, is critical.

However, the other side of the success coin is leadership. Most entrepreneurs do not launch their businesses thinking, "I aspire to be a visionary and great leader." Most times, this is the furthest thing from most entrepreneurs' minds when they are starting out and growing their organizations.

If you're smart enough to put forth all of the energy and effort to solve problem #1 (getting your sales system in place to consistently generate quality leads and convert those to customers, clients, or patients to grow you own income and that of your staff), next you have to tackle problem #2. You must become a visionary leader and a person who sets forth an extraordinary set of ideas and road map about which your staff and those you serve can and will be excited.

You must develop a vision in which your staff will want to invest and get excited about helping you grow your company and dream. In turn, this vision will help them achieve their own goals and the things that matter most in their careers and in their lives. As business owners, we often fail to consider that our dream – the one we're working to get others to rally around – is something in which the team members are investing their own livelihoods. They trust us to run the company in such a way that they can also rely on its health and growth to support them and their own families.

So while becoming a visionary leader may not be at the top of your list as an entrepreneur reading this book (and perhaps it is not even within your realm of focus), it should be. The most important thing I've learned in my years of business and running multiple companies is that the team will ultimately be the thing that makes or breaks the company… and that makes or breaks you.

You'll have to go through many ups and downs, people who are the wrong fit and people who are the right fit, people with both good and bad intentions, and get over many hurdles. It comes with the territory when you are an entrepreneur. All entrepreneurs go through all of these scenarios. It is a misconception to believe that a particular struggle or experience you have with one employee should impact your attitude and overall perceptions around building a team, especially if you had no idea what you were doing as a leader at the time.

Take the time to develop the perfect avatar for your company with the characteristics, values, and attitudes that anyone you hire must reflect. This may seem like a small thing, but as I guide my Legacy Leaders through the process of shedding old employees who did not uphold and reflect

bigger than you.

these things and then bringing in new ones who do, the results are astounding. In fact, one of the members of the program switched out the individuals in one key role and within a month's time netted an extra $40,000 in revenue. It's not magic; it's strategic and it works. The team is behind the dream – remember that always.

I hear and see this from entrepreneurs all the time who have worked diligently for years to get their organizations to a million dollars in revenue and beyond yet are still operating with contractors because they had a "bad experience" with an employee, so they slammed on the team-building brakes and their business growth subsequently slowed or stopped.

They became fearful of the process and fearful of committing to growing into great leaders. You may read that and think, "Wow, isn't a million-dollar business great?!" Sure, it is. But they are missing out on the freedom and fun that should come with running a million-dollar business because basically it's still only them. Trust me, when you're in crisis and you need a fire put out, that contractor across the world to whom you pay pennies on the dollar to cut corners isn't going to be the one to solve it.

The vast majority of businesses could be so much more successful if they pushed through these fears – whether it's the financial investment or managerial responsibility. They are stagnating growth… and disappointed and frustrated with their results. Then they wonder why.

The principle that I always teach is that you cannot expect your team to have a higher level of investment in the business than you do. If you are not invested in them (i.e., making them a full-time, internal employee), you cannot expect them to give you the commitment of a full-time, internal employee. If you aren't willing to give them that opportunity, you should not and cannot expect their full commitment to your company.

As entrepreneurs, we can be guilty of thinking about this in a very one-sided way, focusing only on what we want and need.

The result is business owners who are very disappointed and frustrated that a contractor or part-time employee isn't performing at the same level and with the same commitment as a full-time employee.

At the same time, they fully understand that legally they cannot manage a contractor in the same way they can manage an internal employee. Of course, the results are not going to line up the way they'd like. Think about that for a moment….

It Takes Sales… and Leadership

Growing to become a visionary leader is the path to ultimate wealth and prosperity. It is the path to taking all of your hard work, especially in getting your business to generate leads and convert them, and leveraging it into true entrepreneurial freedom.

Most business owners think that if they address and solve sales problems, they'll be set… that things will be enjoyable and comfortable with them experiencing the freedom of entrepreneurship. They fail to realize that the better they get at generating leads and closing sales, the more their quality of life depends on having a well-run and led team.

Let me repeat: sales and leadership are two sides of the coin when it comes to achieving entrepreneurial success.

bigger than you.

The more you sell and grow, the greater the number of man-hours will be required to serve those clients and fulfill the promises made via your product(s) and/or service(s). If you don't have a team that can market, sell, and produce and serve, every time your business grows, it increases the demand on which you must deliver, whether that's creating the product or delivering a service.

Too many entrepreneurs fail to understand this, let alone embrace it. They are too focused on running the business and its day-to-day operations. As a new business owner, it's very easy to get stuck focusing on getting new clients rather than keeping an eye on the bigger picture.

Let me ask you: "What are you doing today to ensure that three years from now – when all of your efforts come to fruition –you'll have the right infrastructure and people in place to deliver on the promise you made to your clients and your market?"

It is critical for you to keep this in mind and in focus. This is a huge part of being a visionary because starting to think about the team you need **only when** you need it will devastate your business. The process of searching, recruiting, hiring, onboarding, and getting someone up and running in your business can range from three months to a year or longer. Fail to plan and you literally plan to fail.

As I write this book, I know that we will need another sales rep in my coaching company in January (it is now July), so you better believe that the search is starting **now**!

Business growth and success do not solely depend on your ability to generate sales. Many businesses struggle and fail almost as often due to the team structure (not having the right people in the right seats and not having enough of them) as they do to sales failure.

If it doesn't cause outright failure, it is certainly a hurdle to growth. Maybe you've experienced this, and it's come full circle when all of your hard work to grow brings you to the point of an inability to deliver and fulfill the promises made through your company, products, and services... because you don't have the right people in place.

Before reading this book, becoming a visionary leader may not have been part of your own aspirations. However, I hope that if you believe enough in yourself and your business, and you're passionate about your mission in the world and the reason you were put on the planet, that you can and will open your mind to embracing your role – not just as a sales leader but also as a visionary who will build a dream team around you that will sell, market, and produce for you. This is possible in any business type or market.

> *"The quality of a leader is reflected in the standards they set for themselves." ~ Ray Kroc*

We all have the potential and capability to achieve greatness in our fields, but it begins with graduating from being the super employee to the CEO.

If you set the intention to embrace this role as you conclude this chapter, I will give you the exact steps that you must take in the next chapter to begin this amazing journey of increasing your quality of life, getting the ultimate reward from all of your hard work, and having a lot of fun running your business each and every day with a team that is as committed as you are.

Recap:

- The two biggest hurdles to business growth and success are sales and leadership.
- Most entrepreneurs don't set out thinking of themselves as visionary leaders; however, that is the goal to which you must aspire if you truly want your business to deliver freedom.
- Don't expect your team to invest more into the business than you invest in them.
- The more you sell and grow, the more critical it becomes to have a team in place in order to fulfill the man-hours required and keep your quality of life in place.
- When all of your hard work comes to fruition, you want to have the right people in the right seats and have enough of them. Planning for that now is part of being a visionary leader.

Action Items:

1. Rate the degree to which you think of yourself as a visionary leader (1 = Could not be further from my mind; 10 = I have a functioning crystal ball).

2. Rate the level of investment you make in your team (1 = It's a one-way street (after all, I give them a paycheck); 10 = I share a fully complementary relationship with my team in terms of investment by each).

3. Consider the implications of your sales doubling next week or tripling in the next quarter. Assess how prepared you will be and determine who you'll need carrying out various job functions to live up to the promises made by your product(s)/service(s) to your market.

To learn how to put everything we discuss in this book into ***action*** right away, go to www.kellyroachcoaching.com/influence and watch the free, life-changing training now!

Chapter Eight:

Six Pillars of Effective Leadership

Congratulations! You've made it through the trials and tribulations of the mindset part of the book that come with a new way to approach team building and your business. Now it's time to talk about the secret sauce. I'll share the exact recipe that is going to explode your business in the best way possible, allowing you to cash in on what may be years and years of effort on your part, pushing your mission forward in the world and going above and beyond to create a successful business that will stand the test of time.

Now is where we are going to bring together the six core elements of what you need to put in place in the everyday operation of your business to have a dream team that you can trust to:

- Run your business exactly as you would even when you're not there, on vacation, or playing hooky… ☺.
- Treat your clients with white-glove service, no matter what and no matter who's watching because they simply care.
- Put out the fires before they make it to you because they are great at their jobs and will do what it takes to resolve problems with finality in an ethical way that provides a positive outcome for all parties involved.
- Work hard and go above and beyond every day because of how much they care about you

and the business mission, so they'll do everything in the world to not disappoint you.

These are the characteristics, experiences, and feelings that you will enjoy when you implement the six pillars I'm about to teach you.

Before you put the six pillars in place for effective team leadership, the first and most important thing you have to do is lay a foundation on which the six pillars will rest. The foundation allows the pillars to work cohesively together to get your business running like a well-oiled machine. As with any structure, the foundation is critical. The strength of any structure depends on the strength of its foundation. The strength of your business will depend on the strength of the foundation we're about to create.

This foundation is made up of four key components.

Number one is trust. Above all else, if you want people to act in the best interest of your organization and do the right thing, you have to establish a foundation of trust. Your team must truly believe that the decisions you make are not only good for them but are good for your customers and the business overall. They have to know that they can count on what you say. You have to be true to your word. Never underestimate the impact of your relationship with your

> *"Good teams become great ones when the members trust each other enough to surrender the 'me' for the 'we'."* ~ Phil Jackson

bigger than you.

employees. They may not be totally comfortable with their role or that you are asking them to stretch. They may be a bit outside their comfort zone. However, if you want them to do whatever it takes to grow the business, there must be a foundation of trust. If you're pushing them, they have to be certain you have their back. Trust is everything.

Next: communication. Transparency, honesty, and over-communication are core elements that must be present in order to establish a dream team that will stay onboard, working for you and investing their careers with you, and that will ultimately do everything in their power not to disappoint you. I use the term "over-communication" because many times things need to be repeated more than once and because many times failure to have a conversation (perhaps things are not finalized or are still in the works) can actually damage or outright break the trust that has been created. The result is uneasiness and a staff that questions your motives because they don't understand what's happening.

Over-communication means keeping your staff updated on everything going on (relevant to them and their role or impacting them), even if things aren't finalized with a

> *Choose to over-communicate every time rather than risk leaving your team in the dark. The latter quickly erodes trust.*

lot of "maybe's" and loose ends. Even if you are not yet ready to roll something out, still give your staff an indication of it and explanation of why you haven't communicated all the details. ("Hey, we're not quite ready to launch XYZ program and are still finalizing details, but I want to tell you about what is coming and what I know at this point.") Over-communication helps solidify the foundation of trust and keeps your team functioning even if they don't have all of the information.

Take a moment to reflect on your own previous employment situations and both the good and bad that came from communication or a lack thereof. Those instances that made you want to head for the door (and perhaps you did just that) were founded in a lack of trust, a lack of communication, and a lack of transparency.

Failure to communicate with your team, keeping them up to date and allowing them to be part of the process, creates a feeling of disconnect – from you and from the business and its mission. Ultimately, they'll wonder if this is the right environment for them – one that will support them in their own goals. When employees sense a situation of instability, they'll likely embrace the "flight or fight" approach and either leave or become a less-than-stellar team member. Without over-communication, what you perceive to be a minor issue could certainly be a major hurdle for one of your team members, who may quietly begin to look for other opportunities.

When they choose to leave, it seems like "bam – it came out of nowhere" and you're surprised, but the departure is the result of uncertainty that may have been festering in their mind for months. That uncertainty that leads to a new search "in a moment of frustration" could have been prevented completely with better communication!

In order to build an unstoppable dream team, you must continually put yourself in the shoes of your employees and consider how they perceive what is happening around them. Put yourself in the shoes of those ***receiving*** your communication about your decisions. Ask yourself, "If my livelihood was dependent on someone communicating and acting like this, would I feel comfortable investing my future here?"

The third component that goes into building a solid foundation on which the pillars of effective leadership can stand is a mutually beneficial relationship. Your team must see and feel "what's in it for them," and they want to know that your decisions are facilitating their ability to carry out their jobs and serve customers, clients, or patients at the highest level.

Never underestimate how highly invested your team will become in their ability to deliver on the promise to the client! They understand that in the clients' eyes, they represent the business, and in fact, they are the business. Your team is what your clients experience when interacting with your company. Without a doubt, your team is your clients' perception of the business… and your team knows this. As a result, they look to you every day to make decisions that support them in their interactions with clients. When your team perceives that you're making decisions that make it more difficult for them to deliver on the promise or that negatively impact their ability to do their jobs, they're going to lose trust in your leadership and the direction in which the company is headed.

Every successful business has mutually beneficial relationships between the owner and the employees.

I often see this when working with companies that do not have a solid sales system in place. When revenues start to slip (as they invariably will!), company leaders begin to make cuts in areas that then negatively impact the team's ability to carry out their job functions. This becomes a downward spiral of employees leaving, followed by the loss of clients because the team needed to deliver the services (or products) is no longer in place. Ultimately, it unravels completely and ends with layoffs, shut downs, consolidations, business failure. I've seen it all. When I look back at the turn of events, it always comes back to a leadership failure and lack of accountability.

These are exactly the things a great visionary leader should and must think about with every decision. Ask, "Is this a mutually beneficial relationship? Does this decision benefit my clients, my team's ability to carry out their job functions, and my own goals?" There is no reason to compromise one in order to gain the other. There is always a way to generate benefits across the board to serve at a high level, for your employees to serve your clients and for you to be fairly compensated.

Finally, the last part of the foundation is an organization that truly runs like a business. Even extraordinary leadership cannot correct and maintain a business that is dysfunctional, disorganized, and disjointed. I've seen plenty of situations in which extraordinary talent left an organization because it was so dysfunctional in its operations that the talented employee simply couldn't take it any longer. Perhaps, you've been that person. And perhaps, you've lost that talented team member. I'm certain that we've all been caught in this situation at one time or another in our careers.

Neither leadership nor sales alone can solve all issues. There has to be a blueprint for success. In my Legacy Leaders program, a huge part of our energy and focus is on developing the right infrastructure for the organization and understanding what the key positions are that will make it run like a well-oiled machine, ensuring that the right people are aligned with those key positions. Additionally, we review documented processes and how they are implemented to ensure scalability and consistent, effective repetition. This is the core element needed by every organization.

As you are stepping up to become a great leader – which I know that you are because you're reading this book, ready to break through the barriers that may have been holding you back – remember that a business that is built like a house of cards is going to get blown over.

Always keep an eye on infrastructure, making good decisions today that you'll thank yourself for in the weeks, months, and years to come. Again, great leadership and great sales cannot replace a business being "run like a business" with a sound infrastructure to support it!

Now that you understand the four components (trust, communication, mutually beneficial relationships, and a business run like a business) that are required for a solid foundation, let's dive into the six pillars that rest on that foundation for effective leadership and to uncap the talent of the people working for you, so you'll get better results across the board and in every area of your company.

Pillar #1: Training

"Job training empowers people to realize their dreams and improve their lives." ~Sylvia Mathews Burwell

The first and most important component is your training program. Training should have a focused and dedicated set of criteria that you work through with each and every person who comes into your organization, so they develop an expert level of knowledge to perform the job function and full understanding of your culture as well as company mission, vision, and goals.

In many small businesses, this requires both inside and outside training. I can't emphasize this enough. As your business grows, you will begin to hire people for job functions that you've never done before, and you'll be hiring for jobs that no one else in your organization is currently performing. When you do the math on this, you'll quickly realize that you could end up having people training others who have never done the job on which they're training. The result will be the trainee trying to learn from someone who's never performed the task. If this perpetuates, the result can be nothing other than frustration and disappointment on everyone's part.

If you truly care about building a sustainable and scalable business, you must train both internally and externally. Internal training will focus on your mission and vision, how you serve clients, your general systems and processes, the way you do business, and why you do business. Of course, this type of training can only come from within. However, when it comes to more specific tasks within various job descriptions, it will make more sense to use external training for your team (until you have someone at an expert level already doing this role successfully within your organization). In my own case, this has been one of the best investments I've made. Every time I've made an investment in outside training for my team, I've seen substantial growth as a result. Why not use an expert to train your team member for a certain skill and have them learn from the best? This can come in various levels and scopes ranging from a few

bigger than you.

hundred dollars on a course to $15,000 (mastermind, and it has always paid dividends –

When we wait too long to hire and fail to follow up with appropriate and effective training, the result will always be frustration and high turnover rates. If you wait until you hit a crisis, you will likely make a quick hire to get a "warm body in the chair" and then, because you're too busy addressing the crisis, will not dedicate the time needed to effectively train the person.

> *"It is literaly ...
> that you can succeed
> best and quickest by
> helping others to
> succeed."*
> *~ Napoleon Hill*

The new employee is thrown into a fireball of things that need to be done with a haphazard approach on your part. The result will be a need for much cleanup and damage control. "I told the person what needed to be done, so I don't understand how things could have gone so wrong." The reality is that the failure resulted from a poor onboarding process and a lack of investment in the new employee's training and success.

A final training note: The first 30 days of bringing on a new team member will make or break their experience and tenure with your organization. Your onboarding procedure sets the pace, tone, and climate of the role within your organization. It's critical to have the 30-day plan laid out and documented in great detail before you make the hire. When I say "great detail," I mean down to the hour about what they're going to work on both independently and with someone else (you or another team member). It's a common bad habit to bring someone on without having the time to dedicate to their training. The result? The new employee wastes hours waiting on us and gives them an incorrect sense of the pace and climate of the organization. Later, when you want them to accelerate the pace toward a goal, you are going to struggle to get them moving faster and with the sense of urgency you want.

I could write an entire book on effective training (that will come later), but for now, these are the key elements that you need to understand and employ that will be the biggest game changers for you and your new employee.

Pillar #2: Teaching

Give a man to fish, and you'll feed him for a day. Teach a man to fish, and you'll feed him for a lifetime.

We often don't think of ourselves as teachers in our roles as business owners and leaders. However, I've learned over the course of my career that the number one goal of a visionary leader – one who can get people to do things that they didn't think they were capable of, one who gets their team to break records, one who has a team doing things that others only dream of getting their own teams to do – is to develop a love of teaching.

Teaching someone (as opposed to training someone on a particular process or what to do) and focusing on the real understanding of the "why" and gaining a new perspective and insight is both rewarding and critical to becoming an effective leader. In training, you might provide instruction on the mechanics of carrying out a task; however, when you teach, you dive deeper into the reason for the task and how it contributes to the overall organization.

bigger than you.

When you teach, you help someone understand something at its core. You help the employee stretch their thinking and open their mind to various ways to solve problems. Developing your love of teaching is one of the most powerful game changers when it comes to building your unstoppable dream team – one that will do anything for you. When you demonstrate that you are willing to take the time to teach and truly be present with them to help them grow, you are generating mutual reciprocity. Your employee will want to give of themselves in a bigger way and to give more. They'll want to demonstrate that they've "got this" and understand what you are trying to "gift" to them. When you take the time to teach, the resulting gift to the employee is something they will keep with them forever. It goes far beyond learning how to carry out a task.

> *Develop a love of teaching. There is nothing more powerful for a business leader wanting to create a high-performance team.*

What my former boss told me and what I tell my team is that when your manager takes the time to teach and invest in you, the biggest thing you can take away is the learning experience... and that experience is far more valuable than the paycheck. The team member now possesses knowledge, understanding, and perspective that will serve them to achieve what matters to them. A culture of teaching and an understanding of the value of knowledge results in people who are always invested in growing... because you are invested in growing them and yourself. When you invest in growing people, they will invest in growing themselves.

This is very much a culture and mindset. Teaching creates intrinsic value in the relationship between you and your team. This mindset generates their desire to go far above and beyond the "expectations of the job" and help you advance your mission. Since you're reading this, I know that you are already looking for a team that will do far more than simply clock in and clock out at the prescribed 9:00 to 5:00. It takes so much more than that to grow a small company into an enterprise, so nurturing a teaching mindset will serve you well. You have to give what you expect to receive.

Pillar #3: Coaching

"Outstanding leaders go out of their way to boost the self-esteem of their personnel. If people believe in themselves, it's amazing what they can accomplish." ~ *Sam Walton*

Coaching is vastly different from training and teaching. Training helps a person with the mechanical and functional understanding of how to do a task related to their job. Teaching drives the understanding of the "why" and the root. It imparts knowledge, wisdom, and growth-oriented thinking, so they can achieve better results by applying what they've learned – striving for the end goal as opposed to the functional completion of a task.

Coaching is the process of you giving real time, customized, and specific feedback on performance. This is one of the most difficult areas for most entrepreneurs to ingrain in their cultures. Why? Most business owners are still functional producers in their businesses. They're not acting exclusively as leaders. For most reading this book, I believe

bigger than you.

that is probably the case. While your team is doing their work, you're doing yours.

On one hand, this is great because you are likely the top producer in your company. You're pushing the limits to get as much done as you possibly can. That's great. However, when you are so focused on doing your work, you probably aren't listening and watching your team and what they're doing to provide feedback. The result is your team going through their day a bit blindly and possibly making it up as they go along. Mistakes they're making are likely repeated. In my Fortune 500 career and interviewing thousands of candidates, I learned that just because someone did a similar job for a long time doesn't mean they're any good at it! Without coaching, you can actually develop a team of steady employees who may be mediocre or worse at what they do, and they stay because they like working for you. The job may be easy, and they don't receive much structure, pressure, or feedback, so they plod along. They're not actually impactful at what they do, and their efforts are doing nothing for your growth and profitability.

> *Coaching means providing feedback. In order to do so, you must take time to observe what your team is doing.*

You must take time to coach each day or each week, providing feedback on what changes they need to make and making recommendations for them to be more efficient. This can include listening to their phone calls, accompanying them on sales visits, being cc'd on emails, etc. There is no shortage of things on which you can observe, comment, and correct, resulting in you getting faster, more profitable results. I know you have your own responsibilities and can't spend all day, every day observing your team, but ultimately, this should be your goal. Your goal should be to get your team working so efficiently that you can hire more staff. With every hire, you move closer to stepping out of producer role and into the role of visionary leader, in which your primary responsibility is to ensure you have the right people in the right places and performing at their highest level to achieve the growth you want.

One of the best ways to do this is to start somewhere! You don't have to start with several hours a day in observation mode. Instead, start with one day a month, an hour a week, 15 minutes every day to review their emails, or 10 minutes to listen to a phone call. Start from where you are and with what you have, but just get started!

Providing coaching and specific feedback will have a powerful impact on your team's performance... much more so than simply explaining how you want a process to work or why something should be done as you prescribe. Your team actually wants to know not just how to handle *a situation* but how to handle *this situation*. Specific feedback is the only way to address that and guides them on how to improve the next time.

Pillar #4: Mentorship

"A teacher affects eternity; he can never tell where his influence stops." ~ Henry Adams

Mentorship is essential for long-term growth for any person who is striving to become exceptional at what they do. Mentoring can be done with either someone inside or outside of your organization. Having a sounding board in the form of someone with greater knowledge, expertise, and results is one of the most important factors for growth.

It's often difficult to mentor with someone who is the direct supervisor or for an employee to mentor with the business owner. This is especially true when the employee feels that everything they want and need to address may not be appropriate for that particular relationship. On the other hand, in some instances, the business owner is actually the perfect mentor for employees. However, even in this case, as the business grows, you will not be able to be the mentor to everyone.

Start to think about layers in your organization with seniors and juniors, so there is a built-in infrastructure for employees to have someone to look up to, to go to for advice, and to seek help working through issues and concerns. When you're building a team of high achievers, those people will not want to come to you with every question because they fear it could be damaging to their reputation and your opinion of them. (Honestly, you don't want them to.) However, they will want and need some guidance, so you need to ensure the infrastructure is in place to support this.

Turnover is certainly an indicator of the health and success of an organization. Your ability to grow people over time is key to success and cannot be replaced by anything else.

In the same way that "time" on the job without training, teaching, coaching, and mentorship will not necessarily garner results, there is also a knowledge and experience component that only comes with time and can't be shortened.

Retention is one of the most important things that will dictate your business's success and growth rate, and training, teaching, coaching, and mentorship all play a role in retention. Additionally, a lot of this depends on your own mindset.

Are you willing to slow down today in order to accelerate tomorrow? So many entrepreneurs are not willing to do this. They only want to press the accelerator today rather than the brake, so what happens is that they crash and burn tomorrow.

I want you to try on the hat of delayed gratification… at least a little bit of delayed gratification. When you make this mindset shift around becoming an effective leader and start embracing these six pillars, you're setting up a business that can and will grow for decades.

Shortsightedness – only focusing on today – always compromises where you could be tomorrow.

Do you feel that you have the type of relationship with your team in which they view you as an ambassador for them? One who is invested in them and in what is good for them as a person as well as an employee? As a sounding board with an open mind they can approach regarding feedback, suggestions, and struggles?

If you feel that you aren't that person and cannot be that person, how can you help them find the person they need to fill that mentorship role? If you have the capability to be the mentor, begin to wrap your mind around that short-term investment of your time in their growth to get a long-term return in your business.

Pillar #5: Structure

Structure sets you free!

bigger than you.

You may have heard this quote but if you have not yet experienced this, you may not believe it to be true... yet!

I can't emphasize enough that if you crave more freedom in your life, there is nothing more powerful with which to align the free and flexible life you want than structure.

First and foremost, people thrive on structure. One of the biggest misconceptions among entrepreneurs launching their businesses and building teams is that providing structure to the team is the equivalent of micromanagement.

They think it's overbearing when exactly the opposite is true! When people lack structure, they are unproductive coupled with a lack of focus; they struggle and many times fail. Without structure, your team members will not understand exactly what you need done and how you need it done.

The result is friction and frustration between you and your team. A lack of communication is at the root of employer/employee relationships that dissolve and become negative or even adversarial.

The employee becomes frustrated because they don't have a clear road map for success or clear understanding of the requirements coupled with a lack of feedback, so they're never sure when the job is completed and completed well. The employer perceives the employee to be lazy or unproductive, which is often not the case. In reality, the employee is flailing in the middle of the ocean, not

> *People always thrive on structure and clearly communicated expectations.*

knowing what is expected of them and not having the support and structure they need to succeed. This miscommunication and lack of feedback leaves both feeling frustrated, empty... and discouraged. I want to help you fix this in your business... forever.

Every position in your company needs structure and a set of criteria, so everyone has absolute clarity about expectations and everyone can win together. The more structure you provide to your team and the more that structure is upheld every day, the more freedom you will have as the business owner to step back from the day-to-day operations while simultaneously creating a high level of trust with your team.

This trust allows them to operate effectively and efficiently without you – aka more freedom for you. Your team can meet and exceed your expectations because you have systems in place with criteria to define how and why every task should be carried out.

They'll understand the "who, what, why, when, where, and how" of everything they need to do. With ongoing feedback and reiteration, they'll know what's important and what's not. They'll know why things need to be done a specific way and the business implications for doing so. With this clarity and understanding of the why, you will be amazed at the impact even one person can have in creating freedom for you in your business.

Here is a sampling of the things that we help our Legacy Leaders to get systematized in their businesses, and I want you to get started on this now, too!

- Onboarding clients
- Invoicing
- Quality assurance calls

- Revenue-producing job descriptions
- Performance metrics for every role
- Offboarding clients
- Sales and marketing systems
- Customer service and delivery
- Generating consistent lucrative referrals
- Systems for increasing sales conversions

Yes, structure creates freedom, but you must expend the energy and effort to build the systems initially and to keep them maintained. However, with structured systems in place under which your team operates, you can be on the beach in Hawaii while your team stays behind and runs the business for you.

Over the last few years, I have experienced the maturation of my team and the payoff of my efforts to create the structures that support the business now running like a well-oiled machine. As my daughter has gotten older, we've been able to travel more without a need for me to be connected to my computer or my phone. In fact, when traveling, I rarely check in. Everything is run so tightly when I am in the office that the team is crystal clear on what they need to do, so they execute perfectly when I'm not there.

This does not, however, happen automatically or overnight. I always convey to business owners that what they want to enjoy in the future (whether that's six months from now or years from now), they have to begin laying the groundwork and planning for now. For example, when my daughter was born, I knew that our goal for travel as a family would really begin about the time she turned 4-years-old, so I had four years to perfect my team and their ability to run the business without me being in the office.

I'm enjoying that travel freedom now that Madison is four because I planned for it according to my goal's time frame, and that included hiring, training, establishing criteria, building systems, etc.

> *Structure is life changing!*

I knew even before Madison was born over five years ago when I enabled my husband to retire that my goal by the time she went to preschool was to be able to travel the world, take vacations at least quarterly, and sprinkle in a lot of extra mini-getaways in between, and that is exactly where we are today. We are free to do what we want when we want now because I put in place the exact things we have covered in each of the preceding chapters a few years ago and have been working to refine and improve them ever since. Holy hell, is it life changing!

Now it's your turn to get moving today on this life-changing process. I want you to take stock and inventory in your business as you are running it today. Are you working head down on tactical issues just to keep up with the demands of the day? Or are you taking time to look down the road at what you want to achieve and enjoy in the future and strategically making decisions to enable that to happen? Wherever you want to be in one, three, five or more years, you must start to plan now and build out the structure your business needs to operate smoothly and profitably whether or not you're in the office.

No matter how disorganized or disjointed your business may feel or be today, I want you to know that upon reading this chapter, you can get started right now from wherever you are and with whatever you have, just putting one foot in front of the other each day.

It's a building process and it takes time, but it is the key to freedom. Freedom can be engineered into any business in any industry. I wrote this book to help end entrepreneurial burnout forever. I know you have big goals and dreams. You want to scale and grow your business. You want to leverage your efforts to be running your business as a well-oiled machine. All of this is possible and you can do it. Start by looking at your business from 50,000 feet and by making decisions – not just for today and tomorrow – but with an eye on the future and the freedom you want to have and achieve. I assure you: Structure will allow you to grow your business to take care of yourself and your family, to allow you to have the freedom and fun you want, and to advance your mission and make your mark on the world. Just get started!

Pillar #6: Accountability

"The growth and development of people is the highest calling of leadership." ~ Harvey S. Firestone

The final and most important pillar of effective team leadership is – bar none – accountability.

It's the number one thing (besides sales) that entrepreneurs resist. There is a negative connotation around accountability as there is around sales; however, these are two of the most important elements that will help you thrive as a business rather than simply survive. You must have a team that is accountable for sales.

Accountability is simply the discipline to follow through. It encompasses the leader's discipline to require team members to act upon and follow through on what was discussed and agreed to. It is the black-and-white difference between a well-run organization and one that vaguely and loosely gets by for a period of time… until it doesn't.

Every employee needs accountability and structure (as we already covered) to perform at their best. Accountability is the very reason that so many high-achieving CEOs hire coaches and spend tens of thousands of dollars doing so. Even the best of the best, including many of my high-achieving clients, need a coach to hold them accountable.

You see, the CEO role is the only role in any business that has no built-in accountability, and let's be honest: we all need it. As humans, we all have a tendency to slip back into our comfort zones and avoid the very thing we **need** to do, focusing on the thing we **want** to do instead – the thing that's most enjoyable, comfortable, and is the path of least resistance.

Your team will do exactly the same thing if you let them because it's human nature… not because they want to sabotage your success or not because they have bad intentions. Taking the path of least resistance is normal.

Without accountability, your business will struggle and ultimately fail. On the other hand, to build a thriving organization comprised of a team that cares about peak performance, is invested in the success of your firm, and is mature and dedicated, you must hold team members accountable.

Any employee can have the best brought out of them, and become that superstar employee that you are envisioning when these six pillars are in place and put on a firm foundation. If you skip the final pillar – accountability – it's like spending huge amounts of time and money building a custom house on a solid foundation but then never adding the roof. No one would ever move in, and with the first rain storm, all is a waste.

Accountability falls squarely on your shoulders and takes on many forms. It's expecting people to do what they say they're going to do, making sure the business runs on specific metrics on which you follow up weekly and discuss performance against those metrics. It's making certain that employee reviews are done consistently, measuring team members against specific and defined criteria so that every day they know exactly what to do to advance their own careers. In a nutshell, accountability is about requiring people to improve. When mistakes are made or issues arise and you do the necessary training, teaching, and coaching, accountability helps ensure that those mistakes do not occur again.

Accountability is about training your team how to put out fires and deal with issues that arise in the day-to-day operations without having to escalate them to you. It's also about ensuring that you – the business owner – can take a vacation and truly enjoy time disconnected from the business. Once again, this is a topic that could fill an entire book!

It's a misconception to think that accountability must come in the form of harsh criticism or negative, abrasive back-and-forth conversations. That is not what accountability entails. It's about having consistent milestones and check marks along the way that everyone on the team is aware of, agrees to, and that the overall business is measured against. Keep everyone honest and focused – including you – having a road map for the path to your organization's success.

Now you have the exact recipe that I promised at the start of this chapter, this single chapter is one you should re-read as often as you need to because these really are the six steps to building an unstoppable team and enjoying entrepreneurial freedom in any business and in any industry.

Recap:

- You must first have a strong foundation for your business comprised of trust, communication, mutually beneficial relationships, and a business that runs like a business.
- Never underestimate the impact of your relationship with your employees.
- Under-communicating is almost always far more damaging than over-communication.
- Training should have a focused and dedicated set of criteria that you work through with each and every person who comes into your organization, so they develop an expert level of knowledge of their role and an ability to perform the job function fully understanding your culture.
- Want to be a great leader? Develop a love of teaching.
- Coaching is the process of you giving real time, customized, and specific feedback on performance.
- Having a sounding board in the form of someone with greater knowledge, expertise, and results is one of the most important factors to growth.
- Very simply, structure will set you free. Structure is not the same as micromanagement.

> Accountability is the black-and-white difference between a well-run organization and one that vaguely and loosely gets by for a while before it inevitably fails.

Action Items:

1. Look back at your recent communications with your team. How effectively did you communicate? Did you leave loose ends that might be misperceived by your team? Consider how to improve the consistency and effectiveness of your communication.

2. Write down that last few decisions that you made in your business and make note of the degree to which the decision was mutually beneficial. Answer this about each decision: Did this benefit my clients, my team's ability to carry out their job functions, and my own goals?

3. Begin documenting the detailed onboarding process for every role in your organization. Commit to spending at least a few minutes on this each week.

4. Write down the job functions that you need and honestly assess your ability (or that of someone else in your organization) to effectively train for the position. If you've never done it, you will not be able to effectively train someone else.

Six Pillars of Effective Leadership

5. Set aside one day a month (or some other fixed time) to pay attention to what your team is doing (e.g., reviewing emails they send, listening to phone conversations, etc.), so you can provide effective feedback on their performance and determine how they can improve.

6. List the senior and junior roles in your organization and determine how to best match your team members for effective mentorship.

7. List the various areas in your business (e.g., onboarding, invoicing, job descriptions, etc.) and rate the level of detailed structure around them. Also, prioritize those that are most critical to you and schedule time every week to start adding the structure needed, continuing to work your way down your prioritized list.

8. Consider joining and participating in my Legacy Leaders program to get your business running like a business – without dysfunction and disorganization. ☺
www.kellyroachcoaching.com/mastermind

To learn how to put everything we discuss in this book into *action* right away, go to
www.kellyroachcoaching.com/influence
and watch the free, life-changing training now!

Chapter Nine:

The Only Path to True Wealth and Entrepreneurial Freedom

What's on the other side of the entrepreneurial rainbow? What is the pot of gold waiting for each of us when we launch our businesses?

For most, that pot of gold is the freedom to put family first, to build true and lasting wealth, the flexibility to take time for the things you love, and the opportunity to really live out your mission and purpose for being on the planet. These are the most common descriptions I've heard from my clients in eight countries around the world.

I wrote this book because I want to end entrepreneurial burnout. Burnout occurs when everything is on you and you are the business. Now that you've read eight chapters that have taken you on the journey from "being the business" to stepping back and leading the business, you should have a pretty clear assessment of what's going on in your business right now versus what you still need to put into place and make happen in order to cross that rainbow and arrive at your pot of gold.

Honestly, crossing the rainbow is really not that hard. When entrepreneurs can't reach the pot of gold, it's almost always because they didn't even try. (Working hard on the wrong things doesn't count!) As we've covered, there is a negative connotation around hiring, team building, and then accountability, so most business owners simply avoid those processes and are unwilling to take the steps I've outlined in this book.

Since you've made it this far in the book, I know you are in the one percent who are going to make it over the rainbow. You are the one percent who will not only hope for the entrepreneurial freedom and true wealth but will take the action necessary to make it all come together and happen for you.

> *"Management is doing things right; leadership is doing the right thing."* ~ Peter F. Drucker

The Path

The path looks like this: You build a team, so the business's growth does not rely on you working more hours. You then make sure your team is trained to be productive and profitable so that each role within your organization is its own profit center, paying for itself and paving the way for greater profit to make the next hire.

In my Legacy Leaders program, we spend immense amounts of time ensuring that each of the business leaders in the group understands this path and how to carefully construct job descriptions, metrics, and key performance indicators for every position in their organization. With this in place, they can enjoy a solid return on their time and financial investment, not only making an income from every person they hire but leveraging each position to generate the money needed to make the next hire.

bigger than you.

Only when you bring together a team that positively contributes to the bottom line will you be able to create true and lasting financial freedom. This may be a very different perspective on the way you have approached your business from day one. You may not yet see yourself as a visionary leader… or even a CEO. Perhaps it has just been you to this point in your venture or maybe it's been you and a small team that's been acting more like family than employees without structure and accountability. Maybe nothing I've covered in this book to this point reflects where you are today… and that's okay.

Most entrepreneurs get into business because there is something they love – an idea for a product or service that they can bring to the marketplace and the skill set to support that. However, at some point, you have to decide just how badly you want freedom. If freedom – both financial and time – is at the top of your list, then change and growth must become your language of love. When we grow, our businesses grow. When we stagnate, our businesses stagnate.

Imagine the world of possibilities that you can bring to your employees, reflecting back on the foundation and pillars of effective team leadership. Imagine the hidden potential and uncovered opportunity that exists in your business today that you can begin to mine… and monetize… that can increase your impact on the world, grow more systematically, and achieve your ultimate goals.

Sales Skills Matter

I always say (and covered in-depth in my first book, *Unstoppable: 9 Principles for Unlimited Success in Business & Life*) that sales truly is one of the most important life skills for any person who wants to create freedom, flexibility, and financial abundance.

This may be a hurdle in front of you, so it may be difficult to envision yourself teaching and training your team to be productive and profitable if this is not your area of strength. This brings us right back to the idea of the need for external training, and I implore you to get the help you need in order to grow yourself and your team.

Honestly, sales is not an area of strength for most entrepreneurs, but anyone who wants it bad enough can grow and change. It's a matter of asking for help.

You don't need to be the best salesperson in the world in order to effectively manage a well-run sales team, but you do need to learn how to become an effective leader in order to do so. You must be willing to hire people who are passionate about sales, being on the front line and doing whatever it takes to ensure they meet their quotas and objectives that are critical to the firm's success. It's a combination of sales and sales leadership. If you don't excel at the former, you must excel at the latter, and there are countless courses, programs, books, and coaches that are available to help you learn to master sales or learn to master managing and leading a sales team.

If freedom matters to you, make sales leadership your new priority and mantra. Make it your new obsession because truly, your freedom in your business depends on it.

Recap:

> ➢ Reaching the entrepreneurial pot of gold is not that difficult. When business owners fail to reach it, it's almost always because they did not try in

bigger than you.

the first place – or worked too hard on the wrong things.
- You need to make an income from every position in your company and then leverage that position to make enough for the next hire. One position should always be paving the way to the next one.
- If you want greater freedom, you must change and grow.
- Sales is one of the most important life skills for any person who wants to create freedom, flexibility, and financial abundance in their life.

Action Items:

1. Rate your sales skill set (1 = I hate sales and cannot image being a salesperson; 10 = I'm killing it every day.) If you are not at the upper end of this scale, hire a coach or take the steps needed to become the best sales leader possible. Remember that your attitude will be reflected in the behavior and results of your team.

2. Review what you do every day and consider the degree to which you are working very hard… on all the wrong things. Are you spending your time on strategic growth and personal development or tactics that keep you right where you are?

3. Take time to set growth goals for yourself. Remember, when you grow, your business grows.

4. Consider joining and participating in my Legacy Leaders program to better understand the path to entrepreneurial freedom and put yourself on the path more quickly.
www.kellyroachcoaching.com/mastermind

To learn how to put everything we discuss in this book into ***action*** right away, go to
www.kellyroachcoaching.com/influence
and watch the free, life-changing training now!

Chapter Ten:

Transform and Launch!

Now it's time to transform from manager to visionary and catapult your business to become a world-class brand! As you step into the world of entrepreneurship, you are also stepping into the school of hard knocks… and no one can ever truly be prepared for this. I've heard people say that launching and growing a business is the best exercise in which you could ever engage for personal growth. I couldn't agree more.

This journey will at times take you to your knees and at other times have you running up the "Rocky" steps with your arms in the air jumping up and down at the top… and everything in between!

It's an emotional journey. At times, it's a struggle; at times, you'll be filled with joy; and at times, you'll feel like the wind has been knocked out of you, leaving you gasping to take a breath. These high "highs" and low "lows" are worth every ounce of it when you finally bring it all together, allowing you to live the life you know you were put on the planet to live.

There are phases you will go through and you may currently be at phase one, two, or three. In the beginning phase of entrepreneurship, it's all about getting clients. You have to find clients to drive revenue and turn a profit. You have to be able to support yourself. You have to get the business in business and keep it there. In phase two, you build a winning team and surround yourself with people who actually care and are invested in helping you grow the business and scale beyond what you could achieve on your own... hence the book's title: *bigger than you*. Finally, the last step is bringing together your sales system and your team to create a well-oiled machine that self sustains and works for you, so you can arrive at the other side of the entrepreneurial rainbow and enjoy all of the freedom and wealth that comes with that.

The biggest, best piece of advice I have for you as you read this final chapter is to pick your head up and start dreaming again, start playfully imagining and joyfully creating the way you did when you first dreamed about going into business for yourself.

Too many entrepreneurs get stuck in phase one and never advance to phase two. Their head is so far down in the tactics and day-to-day operations (with nose to the proverbial grindstone), always scrambling to put out the next fire and solve the next crisis. They fail to pick their head up to look around and look forward to see how they can evolve and grow and what they might be able to achieve by reaching phases two and three.

What I wish for you is that you recognize whatever big dream you have for your life, however far you want to go, and what you most want to achieve is indeed possible for you. Seek help. Go to any length needed to associate with people who are already where you want to be, are doing what you want to do, and are currently performing at the level you want to achieve.

You will never find an Olympian without a coach. You will never find anyone at the top of their field who is not working with outside counsel on whom they lean heavily to make the right judgement calls when it matters most or to help them grow, develop, and learn through accountability. None of us is exempt. We all have strengths and weaknesses.

bigger than you.

The only way we can bring our life to its pinnacle, to reflect everything we've hoped, dreamed, and envisioned when we began this journey is by getting ourselves into a community of other people who are striving, achieving, pushing, and growing. Put yourself in proximity of greatness and it will rub off... I promise.

The journey of developing a bigger-than-you business is not just about freedom. It's about growth and enjoying the journey along the way. It's about embracing a vision so big for your business and life that you start making decisions today that will impact you and your family five, ten, or 15 years from now. The single biggest mistake I see in the entrepreneurial space is business owners making decisions only for today – get the next client, close the next sale, and stay on top of the latest trend, tool, or tactic. None of these things allows for sustained growth.

I'm certain that none of the huge percentage of business owners who fail actually set out to do so. But I'm also willing to bet that none of those failed business owners made it a point to think like a visionary, act like a true sales leader, and make the decisions we've covered throughout this entire book that are required to build a business that can be sustained and scale.

If you don't ever want to go out and get a job again, you have to make the decisions that will set your business up to last for a lifetime and grow for a lifetime. This is why embracing growth, evolution, leadership, and building an unstoppable team is essential to bring the whole picture full circle and have your business support your life rather than the other way around. I want to challenge you right now to transform from being a task manager, a firefighter who attends to any given daily crisis, and a tactical master to being a visionary. You can be a visionary leader who becomes the go-to expert in your industry or space.

You will deliver at a higher level, execute with more discipline, and build the best team – bar none – that we all know is the deciding factor between success and failure!

I want to challenge you today to take your business from asking, "How am I going to pay the bills and get by this month?" to instead asking yourself: "How am I going to build a world-class brand?" I want you to ask yourself that question every day when you get out of bed: "What am I going to do today to build a world-class brand, a household name, a name synonymous with excellence and timelessness, a name that people know not to haggle with on price or question, doubt, or worry about quality when they engage with you?"

When you begin thinking as a visionary leader and begin making decisions to build a world-class brand, your profitability will go through the roof today and in all the years to come. You won't get caught in the trap into which so many entrepreneurs fall, trying to shortcut the system riding the latest wave or riding the one-trick pony into the sunset… never to be heard from again.

> *"The function of leadership is to produce more leaders, not more followers."* ~ *Ralph Nader*

Every day, I hear complaints from entrepreneurs that the online space is very, very crowded; however, I want to challenge your thinking on this. It's true that there is no barrier to entry and anyone can take their business online.

It's true that you may have dozens, or hundreds, or thousands of competitors, doing exactly what you do, selling and marketing their services online every single day. However, I also want to ask, "How crowded is your space with ***visionary leaders*** who are building a world-class brand? Who set a higher bar for excellence? Create a better set of standards for integrity? Who walk their talk and live, breathe, eat, and sleep what they teach and preach?" The answer to this is: almost none.

Take the principles of this book, take a deep breath, and get ready to charge forward toward your goals and dreams. Ultimately, you have the power and potential to become everything you've dreamed of and so much more. There is almost no one in your space right now who is truly operating at the level of excellence that will be required to take the leadership position. It's yours for the taking right now. That seat at the table is waiting for you!

Recap:

- ➢ Start operating as the captain of the ship, looking forward to the future. Protect and guide your business by being up on top not down below.
- ➢ Start dreaming again and creating the way you did when you first launched your business.
- ➢ You can achieve anything you want, and most big achievers have coaches who help them attain excellence and success.

> Businesses that succeed are the ones being run by visionary leaders, not just tactical managers. Strive to become more and your company will follow.
> When you begin thinking as a visionary leader and begin making decisions to build a world-class brand, your profitability will go through the roof today and in all the years to come.

Action Items:

1. Get started implementing what you learned in this book!

2. Contact me to learn how I can help you in your quest to come the visionary leader you need to be in order to enjoy entrepreneurial freedoms and to build something that is *bigger than you*!

To learn how to put everything we discuss in this book into **action** right away, go to
www.kellyroachcoaching.com/influence
and watch the free, life-changing training now!

Resources

To learn how to put everything we discuss in this book into ***action*** right away, go to
www.kellyroachcoaching.com/influence
and watch the free, life-changing training now!

Attractor Factor cheat sheet: www.kellyroachcoaching.com/attractorfactor

To join my online community of entrepreneurs building their own #biggerthanyou businesses, simply log into Facebook and search for "Tribe of Unstoppables."

To contact my team regarding leadership consulting, transformative business coaching, and speaking inquiries, email: customersupport@kellyroachcoaching.com

Resources

About the Author

Kelly Roach has helped hundreds of individuals master sales, marketing, and business growth strategy to grow their incomes and achieve their goals.

Kelly started her career with a Fortune 500 firm where she was promoted seven times in eight years, becoming the youngest Senior Vice President in the firm. Kelly's experience hiring, training, coaching, and managing individuals across 17 locations up and down the East Coast prepared her for her entrepreneurial journey.

After breaking every record in the company's history for profit, growth, sales, and expansion, coupled with millions in profit added to the bottom line, Kelly knew it was time to focus on helping others do the same.

Kelly's number one passion in life is helping others succeed in business and life with the right strategies, action plan, and mindset for success. Kelly's company, **Kelly Roach Coaching** helps entrepreneurs, business owners, and executive leaders achieve rapid, sustainable business growth in record time. You can learn more about who Kelly is and how she helps people at www.kellyroachcoaching.com.

Kelly does private consulting with corporations, runs online training and coaching programs for entrepreneurs, and hosts her own Elite Mastermind for individuals who are seriously committed to transformative results in their business and life.

Kelly frequently does media appearances and speaking engagements in addition to being the CEO at Kelly Roach Coaching and hosting her weekly podcast,

"Unstoppable Success Radio." Visit iTunes or Stitcher™ to tune in weekly to gain invaluable insights, strategies, resources, and more at:

Unstoppable Success Radio:
On iTunes: www.KellyRoachCoaching.com/iTunes
On Stitcher™: www.stitcher.com/podcast/kelly-roach-coaching/unstoppable-success-radio

Kelly, her husband, Billy, and daughter, Madison, live in West Chester, Pennsylvania with their beagle, Sadie.

Now known internationally as the "Authority for Entrepreneurs and Business Leaders who want more success, freedom, and fulfillment in their lives," Kelly is on a mission to help 1,000,000 people achieve their goals and dreams.

Connect with Kelly:

Facebook: www.facebook.com/kellyroachinternational
Instagram: www.instagram.com/kellyroach13
LinkedIn: www.linkedin.com/in/kellyroachint
Twitter: @kellyroachint

To learn how you can work with Kelly and her team, email coaching@kellyroachcoaching.com or visit www.kellyroachcoaching.com to get in touch with us today.

To order this book as a key resource for an event, seminar, or gifts for clients, simply email customersupport@kellyroachcoaching.com to learn more.

bigger than you.

Hire Kelly to Speak

Kelly speaks nationally and internationally on topics related to entrepreneurial success, leadership, sales mastery, the power of mindset, and how to create unstoppable success in business and in life.

As a former NFL cheerleader turned Fortune 500 executive now Million-Dollar Marketing Mentor, Kelly brings a level of energy, clarity, and passion to the stage that you will be hard-pressed to find elsewhere.

To learn more about booking Kelly for conferences, panels, and team leadership meetings and retreats, visit www.kellyroachcoaching.com/speaking or email speaking@kellyroachcoaching.com.

Hire Kelly to Help You Transform Your Business

Kelly works with clients nationally and internationally in a variety of capacities as a speaker, consultant, and coach.

Kelly's core focus areas include:

- **How to design, build, and grow your seven-figure business online**
- **Rapid, sustainable growth strategies for organizations and entrepreneurs**
- **How to design and build a winning team**
- **Impactful and influential leadership**
- **Sales and marketing strategy and implementation**

About the Author

- **Organizational development and growth planning**

You can email Kelly's team directly at customersupport@kellyroachcoaching.com to learn more about all of Kelly's products and services.

To join Kelly's exclusive email communities and to be the first to receive her trainings, resources, videos and more, visit www.kellyroachcoaching.com.

Acknowledgements

A huge thank you to my amazing family, especially my husband, Billy, my rock, my best friend and confidant. To my amazing team: Thank you for trusting me enough to come on this wild and crazy journey with me. To my mentors (you know who you are): I owe you the world. To Ann, my amazing editor: This project could not have come together without you. And to my clients: You amaze me, wow me and make me unbelievably grateful to be blessed to do the work that I do each and every day – thank you.

~ Kelly Roach

Made in the USA
Columbia, SC
15 January 2023